HOLDING OUR OWN

ALSO BY ANN STANFORD

POETRY

Twelve Poets of the Pacific (edited by Yvor Winters), New Directions, 1937

In Narrow Bound, Alan Swallow, 1943

The White Bird, Alan Swallow, 1949

Magellan: A Poem to Be Read by Several Voices, Talisman Press, 1958

The Weathercock, The Viking Press, 1966

The Descent, The Viking Press, 1970

Climbing Up to Light, The Magpie Press, 1973

In Mediterranean Air, The Viking Press, 1977

The Countess of Forlì, Orirana Press, 1985

Dreaming the Garden, Cahuenga Press, 2000

TRANSLATION

The Bhagavad Gita, Herder and Herder, 1970

EDITOR

The Women Poets in English, McGraw-Hill, 1972

Critical Essays on Anne Bradstreet (coedited with Pattie Cowell),
    G.K. Hall, 1983

CRITICISM

Anne Bradstreet, the Worldy Puritan: An Introduction to Her Poetry,
    Burt Franklin, 1974

Holding Our Own

THE SELECTED POEMS OF

Ann Stanford

Edited by
Maxine Scates
& David Trinidad

Copper
Canyon
Press

Poems in this collection were previously published in the following volumes: *The Weathercock* (The Viking Press, 1966); *The Descent* (The Viking Press, 1970); *In Mediterranean Air* (The Viking Press, 1977); and *Dreaming the Garden* (Cahuenga Press, 2000).

Introduction copyright 2001 by Maxine Scates and introduction copyright 2001 by David Trinidad

Portions of Maxine Scates's introduction appeared originally in *Poetry East* and *The Writer's Chronicle*.

Printed in the United States of America.

The editors wish to thank Bill Cadbury, Rosanna Norton, and Carol Muske for their support.

Grateful acknowledgment is made to The Easton Gallery for the use of *Evening Palm* by Arturo Tello on the cover.

Copper Canyon Press is in residence under the auspices of the Centrum Foundation at Fort Worden State Park in Port Townsend, Washington. Centrum sponsors artist residencies, education workshops for Washington State students and teachers, blues, jazz, and fiddle tunes festivals, classical music performances, and The Port Townsend Writers' Conference.

LIBRARY OF CONGRESS CATALOGING-IN-PUBLICATION DATA

Stanford, Ann
Holding our own: the selected poems of Ann Stanford / edited by Maxine Scates and David Trinidad
   p. cm.
ISBN 1-55659-158-6 (alk. paper)
I. Scates, Maxine. II. Trinidad, David, 1953–   . III. Title.
PS3537.T1815 A6 2001
811'.54– DC21   2001001016

9 8 7 6 5 4 3 2 FIRST PRINTING

COPPER CANYON PRESS
Post Office Box 271
Port Townsend, Washington 98368
www.coppercanyonpress.org

CONTENTS

from *Dreaming the Garden* / 2000

HOLDING OUR OWN

"Of heat and orchards
and sweet springing places"

"I took a walk up the hill and around a bit this evening.... It is not as good as a real country walk, but rather interesting, with the houses built right at the edge of the street, and close together, almost like a big apartment house and in between, the chaparral still grows — sumac trees, and sage, with its lavender orbs now in bloom, and a few sunflowers. Things smell good and woodsy. And on the high part of the hill, I could look down and see the fog coming in, coming across the street, and drifting up over the embankments." So wrote Ann Stanford in a 1954 journal entry as she located herself in a scene very Californian, for the hill she described was not part of the miscellany of just any landscape but rather a hill in Los Angeles, whose environs have so often suggested a place of both fecundity and loss, a place where the unnatural imposes itself on the natural with sometimes disastrous results — and indeed, Ann Stanford was a poet whose poetry was both grounded in place and haunted by its erosion.

I first read Ann Stanford's poetry in the form of *The Weathercock* and *The Descent* when I was about to be her student at California State University, Northridge, then San Fernando Valley State College, in 1970. When I turn to these poems now, I understand once again how they are always with me, as the lines come back to me, familiar, the bedrock of my consciousness. These were poems which welcomed admission to and ultimately defined a world of poetry that I then desired yet knew nothing about. And though it is the work, rather than the teacher, I am about to introduce, I have to note that at age twenty the two were inseparable for me and this, I think, is not an unimportant point. I remember how hungry I was to write, to be heard, to be a poet, whatever that meant, but I was also wordless, intimidated by the teachers, all male, I had thus far encountered. I needed a woman teacher and I had found one, which, in and of itself, was still a rarity at that time in the California schools. And so, a student who had only recently gained reentry to school after having flunked out, I bought the books of the *woman* poet whose classes I could not yet get into. I wanted to know what poetry held for me, and the point that seems crucial to make is that I would not have found out had poetry not been made real for me by the quiet yet direct presence of that woman who stood in front of the class.

These were the interests I brought to her work. I had found a poet who I believed would teach me, and now I needed to find the idea of poetry in her work. Though I was an English major, I was still a neophyte reader of poetry, but now I had the books in my hands. It was the spring of Cambodia, of Kent State, of Jackson State, and early in May I was a follower in the halls, in the administration building, a participant in demonstrations that eventually shut the school down. I had a job in Wyoming that summer, fleeing the rage that I had encountered both in the halls and in myself, and I took *The Weathercock* and *The Descent* with me — hence the encounter with both books now seems simultaneous.

I read *The Weathercock* and *The Descent* over and over that summer. At first I was drawn to their clear-sightedness, a lucidity which then and now seems to be straightforwardly radiant. "The earnest part / Of heat and orchards and sweet springing places. / Here I am printed with the earth / Always and always the earth ground into the fingers" — how I loved and love those lines from "The Blackberry Thicket." Through them I think I first understood narrative, the catalytic moment-story of the poem that both names and gives rise to feeling. Moreover, in this poem I found the heart of many of Stanford's thematic concerns. The book jacket of *The Weathercock* called her a "California poet," and those orchards then and now tell me of the longing for shade, those "sweet springing places" from which her poetry comes.

So it was not only the fact of the teacher, but also the fact of the place that would come to matter for me. Though when I knew her she lived at the top of Benedict Canyon in a house she and her husband had built (where in my senior year, much to my awe, she conducted a poetry workshop consisting of a group of us she had specially selected), she had been raised in the country south of Los Angeles which had more recently given way to the inevitable sprawl of post–World War II housing tracts. These lines from "Done With" (from *The Descent*) speak to and reclaim that breathing and not so distant past:

> They are trampling the garden —
> My mother's lilac, my father's grapevine,
> The freesias, the jonquils, the grasses.
> Hot asphalt goes down
> Over the torn stems, and hardens.
>
> What will they do in springtime
> Those bulbs and stems groping upward
> That drown in earth under the paving,
> Thick with sap, pale in the dark
> As they try the unrolling of green.
>
> May they double themselves
> Pushing together up to the sunlight,
> May they break through the seal stretched above them
> Open and flower and cry we are living.

In such lines I recognized something that I knew, but could not yet articulate. I had grown up in one of those housing tracts laid over a beanfield a mile from L.A. International Airport, a landscape of placelessness. But in her work I heard the echo of something that was still in the wind, voices whispering, something I had been told, a layering of sound that spoke of more natural landscapes beyond the jets and sprawling freeways as in the last lines of "The White Horse": *"Where is the white horse, I said, / She was here yesterday."* These landscapes, that "yesterday," had existed in my mother's memory as well, for she was Stanford's age. And though my mother had not grown up in the country but in downtown Los Angeles, she had taken car rides to the country with her grandparents and told me of those Sundays when her grandmother picked wild mustard for the birds. I had rarely seen that countryside myself since one had to go farther and farther to find it, but I was now hearing my mother's stories of that lost countryside in Stanford's work. As well, I think these poems suggested to me that it was possible to name what one had barely heard, what one might only suspect — and, of course, as I see now in a most wonderful way they also corroborated my mother's memories, validating them as one woman, across the boundaries of class and education, gave another woman's story back. Thus, these poems coincided with my own desire to recall memories that had seemed groundless, perhaps by the very nature of that unreferenced placelessness, and certainly because, though I may have felt the desire, I had not seen how to make anything of my own or my mother's story, stories that had seemed filled with only loss.

What I was coming to understand about poetry's ability to name came precisely from the fact that these voices, so much a part of her work, did echo and mutter over a lost landscape with something more than hazy nostalgia. Diamond-edged, poems such as "Pandora" embodied not only loss but the admission that erosion and the ensuing exile brought on by change was heartbreakingly inevitable. And if at first I had been drawn by the clarity with which she created the natural world, if not the historical, where the Spanish place-names I mispronounced spoke of yet another history I had not learned in school, I was soon drawn to the nature of the poet's exile from that world, most specifically in the ways her poetry embodied that exile in relation to the making of poetry in the last lines from "The Walnuts":

> There the grove, hanging forever real in the air.
> And I an exile, knowing every turn
> And turning home, and lost in the dazzled road
> The strange, swept premises, and the great trees gone.

Stanford was teaching me a difficult lesson, perhaps the most important lesson I would learn from her work, though surely not one I could have articulated then.

For in these poems there was not just loss, or vulnerability in the face of the erosion of place, there was also the resistant nature of the poem "hanging forever real in the air." Not only did this exile reclaim what was seemingly lost by naming that natural world, she constructed a new world, a metaphysical landscape with the same lucidity — and, as we see in the following lines from "The Organization of Space," in that construct lies the sustaining possibility of the poem:

> And yet a vacancy, an almost none,
> An arching of the mind into a sky
> Under which empty fields and barrens lie,
>
> A round of almost gone, a black and sere,
> Returns across the vivid local tiers
> And turns them to a round, unshaded sea.
>
> Spirit or being, corn-god or harvester,
> That sets us deep within the year's concern,
> Hold the circumference in which we turn.

Reading these poems, I could begin to see not only that what *was* might be remade, but that even if the perimeters of the natural world seemed to collapse there could be something beyond that collapse. There was the possibility of the poem maintaining something essential of that world, a remaking which occurred as the poet created a "circumference in which we turn" that, in turn, formed the integrity of the poem's landscape as she inhabited both the vista and "the almost none" and made both *here*.

It was the "almost none" that was hardest for me to comprehend, and, of course, it was the astonishing clarity with which it was depicted that made that dawning comprehension at all possible in the first place. I suspect the comprehension of what "almost none" truly meant came much later, possibly because it suggested a kind of evenhandedness that seemed to deny the possibility of joyfulness when I was looking for joy in poetry, a joy which I imagined in easy answers rather than existential acknowledgment. But even then in that evenhandedness I think I was beginning to understand that poetry was not a defense but a making. Constructed out of both past and present, Stanford's poetry acknowledges what *was*, what *is* "till vacantness is lost."

This sense dominates *In Mediterranean Air*, the last of her books from Viking[†], while further articulating the vulnerability of the home space where change seems to loom as an ominous intruder on the horizon, where, as she writes in these lines from "Prophet": "Ravens flew by sometimes. Small groups of men / he shouted to, came, bringing others. / Clearly the world couldn't go on like this." It is exactly her ability to address both the

---

† In light of variant spellings in the Viking volumes and in the *Dreaming the Garden* manuscript, my coeditor, David Trinidad, and I have honored Ann Stanford's usage in *In Mediterranean Air*, which was the last volume published during her lifetime. With "Returning Once More" and "The Old Couple" we opted for versions published in magazines, namely *The Southern Review* and *Poetry*.

inevitability of change and the world lost to it, the locus of place and erosion of place, which further defines the sense that the world would go on exactly like this: "And I keep thinking of the balance of things / and how we might change should they settle among us" (from "The Four Horsemen"). Indeed, it is "the balance of things" that becomes an abiding concern as, like the prophet, she continues to suggest we must make what we can of the world.

She reinvents that notion in her last collection, *Dreaming the Garden*, which is dominated by the title sequence where the *idea* of the garden and whatever dreams we have for it are central. In this sequence she explores the ways in which we would tame the natural world by selecting elements from it that in turn form the merely symbolic; yet the ornamental, she suggests, does not account for either natural or unnatural disasters that do take place. Here her poetry of inevitable exile from the garden takes its final and luminous shape as the attempted garden is reclaimed by the natural world. In part nine, "Deserted Garden," she reminds us that "This garden needs you" and we, by turn, need it. But which garden do we need? She answers at the conclusion of the sequence:

> You are the garden. Let it circle around you.
> You are the heart of the maze, where the laurel
> draws its own pyramid, shakes out its limbs
> overhangs the path and takes the form of trees.

I take her to mean that the garden that survives is one in which we tend the necessary, rather than smothering it with artifice. And, for me, this is the essence, the living, breathing beauty of Ann Stanford's poetry — its prismatic and dazzling clarity.

It's been thirty years since I first read Ann's poetry, since I was first drawn into the current her poems named. How lucky I was to have these poems, this teacher, and then friend, whose generosity and encouragement changed my life. How pleased I am that these poems are again in print so that others may learn from them as I did. When I think of her I recall the unassuming directness that characterized her relation to her work and to her students. I recall how she once warned me against expecting too much from poetry, though, of course, I could not take that warning seriously precisely because her work had already promised so much. She taught me that it was possible to take what was without within in order to make it flow congruently from the inner being that is poetry. In "such centering" I understood the possibility of the poem becoming the site of incontrovertible sustenance even as it depicted the fleeting nature of what it sustains: "Transparent, then, and gone like water / Floating off, yet here…." And finally, forever in her debt, I understood the nature of that first moment when we are beyond ourselves, joined to that joyful pursuit of voices just beyond what we can hear.

Maxine Scates

Holding Her Own

When she died in 1987, at the age of seventy, Ann Stanford was at the apex of a long and distinguished career as a poet, translator, editor, scholar, and teacher. Over a period of forty years, she had written eight volumes of poetry, two verse plays, and a book-length study of the Puritan poet Anne Bradstreet. She had also translated the classic Sanskrit text *The Bhagavad Gita* and edited *The Women Poets in English*, an anthology that gathered, for the first time, hundreds of years of poetry by women. Her poems had appeared regularly in the most prestigious journals and magazines — *The New Yorker, The Atlantic, Poetry, The New Republic, The Southern Review* — and had been widely honored. She had received two NEA grants, a Pushcart Prize, the Shelley Memorial Award, the National Institute of Arts and Letters Award for Literature, numerous Borestone Mountain Poetry Awards (the *Best American Poetry* of its day), the Di Castagnola Award from the Poetry Society of America, and many other accolades. Stanford's first priority was always her work; recognition found her as she dedicatedly, and humbly, pursued it. That she achieved as much as she did while at the same time raising four children, earning a Ph.D., and teaching literature and writing at California State University at Northridge during the turbulent sixties and seventies, is a testament to her energy and to her determination. And that she was able to accomplish it all in her native California, far from the literary center of the east, is as admirable as it is inspiring.

It might have been reasonable to assume, given her spectacular track record, that Ann Stanford had secured a place in American letters. But as she herself observed, "nothing is changeless." (Impermanence is, in fact, one of her major themes.) With the exception of *The Countess of Forlì*, a verse play written in the fifties, which was published in limited edition in 1985, Stanford died with her poetry out of print. She'd completed a new manuscript, *Dreaming the Garden*, but had been unable to place it. (The Viking Press, publisher of her three previous collections, turned it down after Stanford's editor there left.) A selected poems she had compiled, *The Skyrocket*, also went unpublished. Had her friend and supporter May Swenson not died shortly after Stanford, she might have helped see these last manuscripts into print. Stanford's papers were donated to the Huntington Library (per her wishes; she had been their poetry consultant for many years) and a strange stony silence set in.

For the longest time, it appeared as if Stanford's entire life's work had been reduced to a blip in the voluminous *One Art*, Elizabeth Bishop's selected letters. In 1971, when Bishop refused to be included in *The Women Poets in English*, May Swenson tried to convince her otherwise, to no avail. In a letter responding to Swenson's plea, Bishop said that she thought the project, which Stanford had worked on for at least fifteen years, "silly & wrong." Peeved, Swenson wrote to Stanford (I quote from an unpublished letter in the Stanford archive at the Huntington): "That E.B. is such a p _ _ _ k in a way. Well, I guess she's just eccentric." (Undoubtedly foreseeing a day when someone would repeat her words, as I am now, Swenson coyly encoded her slur.) After her death, of course, Bishop's work would be published in a number of all-female anthologies; she was no longer there to resist, as she had when approached by Stanford, in such a condescending manner: "Why not *Men Poets in English?*"

Although it came out in the midst of the women's movement, Stanford's anthology failed to click in a way it, perhaps, should have. Reviewing *The Women Poets in English* in the

New York Times Book Review, Adrienne Rich devoted the better part of a full page to her own assessment of the plight of women writers; only in her final sentence did she deem, almost begrudgingly, Stanford's fifteen-year effort a "breaking of ground." Other critics were quick to acknowledge Stanford's "sterling scholarship." In the *Los Angeles Times*, Carolyn See wrote: "[T]his new book, although it probably owes its publication to the current fashionableness of the women's movement, is obviously not the product of a mind swayed by fashion." See also praised one of Stanford's poems, the physically violent "The Beating," as "single-handedly... refut[ing] every lady-like, lacy tradition attributed to women." Still, Stanford's work was not included in two anthologies that soon followed her own, *No More Masks!* and *Rising Tides*, even though both focused exclusively on American women poets of the twentieth century.

Why the neglect? As noted as she was, it's clear that Ann Stanford — while she was alive and during the thirteen years since her death — has had to take a backseat to more relevant poets: Rukeyser, Brooks, Levertov, Rich, Sexton, Plath. Perhaps Stanford's voice is too quiet, too unassuming to attract, as Dickinson put it, "an admiring Bog." Her poems are neither overtly political nor confessional, both crowd-pleasing properties when Stanford was in her prime. Twenty years ago, Joan Johnstone suggested that Stanford's work was anchored in "feminist concerns of long tenure," versus more transient political issues. Carol Muske, writing recently about Stanford's neglect, affirms Johnstone's notion of longevity: Stanford's poems, she says, "were written to last." Stanford, more patient than discouraged, summed up her own predicament in "The Weathercock": "I crow though none may hear. / In the vast spinning world, I still point true."

As is often the case, Stanford found it necessary to cast off her initial influences in order to evolve into a mature artist. Her earliest poems (published in the 1940s by Alan Swallow's eponymous legendary small press) were composed in the shadow of a stern mentor, Yvor Winters, and seem archaic and constrained compared to the more lucid style she developed in the decades that followed. Though she would abandon the predictable rhythms and rhymes of these first efforts, her concerns, for the most part, would stay the same: the orchards of her childhood remembered as a mythical garden; man's relationship to, and invasion of, nature; the acceleration of modern life. Eventually, a clean, agile, and penetrating line replaced the conventional diction of her youth. Stanford admired William Carlos Williams and H.D., and learned much from them about the "vigor and accuracy of the imagination," about clarity of image. Kenneth Rexroth called Stanford's streamlined quality "crystalline" and "illuminating." By refining her language, she was able to break free of Winters's restrictive formalism and assert her independence as a poet.

Stanford had already undergone this aesthetic transformation by the time the sixties, and their attendant turmoil, arrived. As an artist she made use of the prevailing energy, but no matter how much her world changed, Stanford remained true to her individual principles. An indomitable voice, she speaks from the center of intense historical, personal, and artistic flux, her vision as fixed as her weathercock, a fully conscious, unflinching "eye." This "calm at the center of the storm" motif, which runs throughout her work, is superbly rendered in "Glimmerglass," a poem inspired by James Fenimore Cooper's *The Deerslayer*:

> Outside the ring — the house, the lake, the shore —
> The unbroken forest. There the enemy waits
> Circling and stalking the house in the center.

Round within round to the very eye
That watches from the knothole, the heart that hides
In the house in the lake in the circle of the forest.

Stanford's eye may be "dark" — preoccupied with the perils and inevitabilities of human existence — but it is balanced by an acceptance (and often celebration) of the vicissitudes of nature and a belief in the integrity of the spirit, particularly when manifest in an artist's design — be it a garden, a painting, a collection of seashells, or a swordmaker's blade. In a way, at all times Stanford has her eye on change. "If we should change / Is not this the season?" she asks in "Metamorphosis." Her rhetorical question echoes Charles Olson's empowering "will to change" dictum, though Stanford's intention, in context, is to abide the natural order of things, honoring an organic — rather than self-imposed — turmoil.

The span of Stanford's body of work shows what the middle fifty years of the twentieth century (roughly 1935–1985) looked like to a clear-sighted, stable American poet. She bears witness to the cost of progress: intimacy with the earth forsaken for the expediency of air travel, the wildness of her beloved Southern California rapidly vanishing beneath concrete. This is a poet who tells us what is coming by reporting what is being lost. When, at the end of "The Walnuts," she states, "the great trees gone," her words carry the weight of an oracular pronouncement: the era of majestic personalities has passed. In "On the Death of the President," she responds instantly, and lyrically, to the most significant historical event of her time: the assassination of John F. Kennedy. "The country gathers toward noon in the midst of the country," she laments, commemorating a moment from which America will never recover; the future, from that point forward, is a "darkening field." The last two lines of a more personal elegy, "Going Away," seem to prefigure our own increasingly isolated, computer-dominated lives: "We will go back into our houses / We will forget how large the world was once."

One of the most sustaining qualities of Stanford's vision is her archetypal interpretation of the major political currents of the day. Again and again, Stanford absorbs the temporal and recasts it, via her classical imagination, into more indelible, often mythic forms. In reaction to the 1970 student shootings at Kent State, she wrote "Our Town," an ominous little parable about the prototypical, morally upright American village. Here, the horror of war, hitherto a distant, abstract reality, disrupts the town's peaceful (read: numb) existence. The poem's title and its formally antiquated quatrains perfectly mirror the rigidity of the townspeople, which is shattered by the resounding gunshots in the final line. Even before Kent State, Stanford had looked to the past (in "American Tragedy," her poem based on Philip Evergood's painting of Chicago's infamous 1937 Memorial Day Incident, which left ten striking steel workers dead) to find an equivalent to growing civil unrest. When asked to contribute to *Poetry* magazine's anti-war issue in the early seventies, Stanford submitted "The Burning of Ilium," one of her translations from Euripides' *The Trojan Women:* "… our country perishes…. you will merge with the dear earth, without a name." And she employed a chorus of mythical personae ("The Women of Perseus") to unfold an age-old narrative of female subordination — no doubt her response, if not her allegiance, to the then prevalent women's movement. Stanford sees *through* history: "End and beginning and end, forever and ever." She's wise enough to know that whatever has happened "must be done all over again," and to know that, as she reads and writes, "the slow fire of hours / darkens the pages."

Late in life, Stanford's work became even more lucent and stripped-down, free of the least excess. Her last poems seem absolutely effortless. "There's left only me," she says in "Mind,"

"Out of myself the clean thread —" At the end of a consummate career, the artist inhabits her creations completely. She is no longer a poet writing *about* a garden, she *is* the garden: "… it takes your form. / It is real now, not a plan, not even a vista, / but a warm wall in winter.…" She is no longer the maker, she is the bell, "where the sound comes to birth." She is no longer the discrete storyteller, she is a participant in her own myths — although hers aren't any less fateful than traditional tales. Her old couple is unprepared for prominence, her goat dancer is nostalgic for an "enchanted" past, her island woman is alone. Yet Stanford is well attended: she has her poems — hundreds of them — and they are agreeable "traveling companions" indeed.

I didn't know who Ann Stanford was when, in 1972, a freshman at Cal State, Northridge, I enrolled in her Introduction to Literature class. Only later did I learn she was a poet, and a nationally known poet at that. Though I had dreamed of becoming a writer, I had no idea what direction my life would or should take. A high-strung eighteen-year-old, I was too terrified of the judgment of others to speak in class; I sat there intensely, taking it all in. Writing (and especially writing "for" Ann) was the one place I seemed to be able to express myself without undue fear of condemnation. Ann noticed a spark of talent in me, and her encouragement (minimal really, though it felt monumental at the time) altered the course of my life. I would study with her on and off — both independently and in poetry workshops — until I graduated from Northridge.

My memories of my college years center largely upon her. I frequently visited her office (situated on the eighth floor of Sierra Tower, a structure similar in shape to the monolith in 2001: A *Space Odyssey*) to discuss my poems. Just as often, I'd walk past her open door simply to catch a glimpse of her or to say hello in passing. (Other students, I discovered, lurked about the hallway for that same purpose.) She was always patient and kind (though appalled by my poor spelling). I felt calm, accepted in her presence. It was enough that she said she liked a poem. Her suggestions, I recall, were seldom extensive. She'd write her neat, succinct comments in pencil; once alone, I'd scrutinize her jottings with pride.

It's strange to think that Ann was in her midfifties when I first knew her, still ten years older than I am now. She had a full head of graying hair; a lilting, "happy" voice; and a hint (it always struck me) of Asia in her features. In a poem I wrote to her in 1975, while attending one of her workshops, I describe her as "exquisitely wizened, strong." I describe her relaxed manner of dress: "crepe blouse, plaid slacks, casual shoes." And I describe her positive effect on students as "the lithe shadow of wise wings" gliding across "fragile crops." (Excuse my youthful embellishment!) She chose her words carefully, was considerate yet firm; she'd gently override one of us in order to make an important point. I seem to also remember an occasional pained expression, which prompted me to imagine that she would rather have been off somewhere else, doing something more useful or exciting, or that she was experiencing the limitations of a job she was "too big" for. In later years, when I saw her at book parties and readings — a glass of white wine in hand, her demeanor open and warm — she embraced me affectionately, as a friend.

From the teacher I learned valuable skills, but from the poet I gained insight, access to mysterious truths. Her poems told me — so green, so naive — what growing old would be like: that it *would* one day come, and that it would feel sudden: "I woke. And I was old." Freshness would fade ("the day crumpled and worn / Like a picture handled too much"); there would be mistrust, indecision. Continual loss. Things we cherish disappear. Cities topple. Libraries burn. Despite all that, her poems say, the journey is worth it. Discipline ("a practiced waywarding") and ethics ("*Do what you can* and *Take heart*") are the basis of a "clear existence," one in which "depth [is] the clean repeating of / The seen." Hers is Frost's less-traveled road. Ann already knew where the other road led: "Poor simple fellow. Is that all your depth? / I have a poem here that's so profound / No one can understand it but myself." How fortunate for Ann that May Swenson, a peer whom she respected, was capable of articulating her achievement. "The beauty of your work," Swenson wrote Ann at the very end of her life, "is its clean simplicity, of image, sound, message woven together without artifice, to convey pure emotion to the reader. Pure emotion is poetry's task. It has become very rare among us."

As a student of Ann's, I would never have dreamed that I would one day coedit her selected poems. In the early nineties, a writing student of my own, Meg Daly, introduced me to the work of Maxine Scates, who had been her teacher at Lewis and Clark College in Oregon. From Scates's poem "The Teacher," I learned that she too had studied with, and been profoundly affected by, Ann. Students and teachers, weaving a cloth, like Ann's "maker," that "will not fade." So it was Maxine I would later contact to discuss Ann's out-of-print status. Not surprisingly, this subject was also on Maxine's mind. Thus we decided to team up and, with the blessing of Ann's daughter Rosanna Norton, edit the present volume. We combined our own choices with many poems from *The Skyrocket*, the selected manuscript that Ann had prepared, and adopted a title that we hoped would better signify the enduring quality of the work. We chose not to include any of Ann's early poems — her mature voice clearly begins with the first poem in *The Weathercock*, "The

Blackberry Thicket." We also chose not to include any translations or excerpts from her verse plays, but to concentrate solely on the poems in her four major collections.

Some recent events indicate a renewed interest in Ann's work. *Dreaming the Garden,* her manuscript of final poems, was issued by Cahuenga Press, a Los Angeles poets cooperative that includes another former student of Ann's, Harry Northup. Carol Muske and Maxine Scates have written a feature on Ann in the Associated Writing Programs *Writer's Chronicle.* And of course Copper Canyon Press is publishing *Holding Our Own,* which makes the full range of Ann's gift available to a fresh audience. I believe there is a need for her distinct, rational voice. For almost thirty years I have been braced by these poems, have lived by such lines as "I am caught between never and now" and "nothing here finished yet." I rejoice that Ann has made it into this new century. It's obvious she will continue to hold her own.

David Trinidad

FROM

The Weathercock

1966

The Blackberry Thicket

I stand here in the ditch, my feet on a rock in the water,
Head-deep in a coppice of thorns,
Picking wild blackberries,
Watching the juice-dark rivulet run
Over my fingers, marking the lines and the whorls,
Remembering stains —
The blue of mulberry on the tongue
Brown fingers after walnut husking,
And the green smudge of grass —
The earnest part
Of heat and orchards and sweet springing places.
Here I am printed with the earth
Always and always the earth ground into the fingers,
And the arm scratched in thickets of spiders.
Over the marshy water the cicada rustles,
A runner snaps sharp into place.
The dry leaves are a presence,
A companion that follows up under the trees of the orchard
Repeating my footsteps. I stop to listen.
Surely not alone
I stand in this quiet in the shadow
Under a roof of bees.

The Riders

For Eunice

We made castles of grass, green halls, enormous stem-lined
    rooms
And sailed in trees.
Close to the backyard fence
We dug a cave.
We never finished it,
But there was plenty of time for moving that last foot or two
    of earth,
It was an eternity till Christmas.

Do you remember the yellow fields
We tussled through, small mustard petals clinging?
And the hikes on Saturday up to the grove of oaks?
Plenty of time then, and dark came down before we were home.
They were out calling and searching.

There was a winter year and a summer year.
The last was for beaches.
Salt wind over the gaudy pier,
And things moved faster.
You on the yellow horse, I on the dun.
One way the sea, the battleship,
The pier, the fishers leaning by the rail,
The ferris wheel,
And turning still
The shoddy mermaid painted on the wall.
Up and down we laughed and caught the rings.
And one was gold for summer.

Then summer was gone, and the horse bunched warm ripples
Trotting through orchards down to the practice ring.
His eyes were like suns, when he changed his gait
Faster and faster till the trees blurred and the sky
And there were only posts and the wind and the packed earth
And the warm beast gathering and springing.
How to get off, how to escape!
At last I fell, but it was no better.

The earth turned under my back
Swift, swift, we turned out of day to night to day again,
Light and shadow from a picket fence.

And the planet whirled on the sun, a swift carousel.

Our heads grow grey, our children laugh in the long grasses.

Union Station

There was a feather in her hat.
Smiling and waving as the great wheels turned,
Calling *Good-by, Grandmother,* we caught last sight of her.
But in the grey cavern of the terminal
She is a part of every parting.
These things accumulate —
The cheerful cries
For untold years of summer-passing aunts;
College vacations; father walking slow.

They travel trains unseen and mythical
Each followed by his ghostly fellow-riders.
Sudden as tears they come around the ramp
Running the gauntlet of the waiting room.
For this they bought
Their long tickets, locked their doors on dust,
Jogged out of every-morning to this moment
This precise place, this point of meeting
Solemn and arched as a cathedral,
Here where we waited, planning the ambuscade.

The plane makes travel nothing, and the steamer
Beckons a party or a sun-pithed palace.
But here it is we learn the weight of travel.
It is time spent observing distances
Seen through blurred glass, felt in the jolting road,
Conforming to earth's curving hills and passes,
Waiting, strange faces, crowds, and memories hanging
Like posters on the walls beneath the windows.

Small Garden

Stout wall and careful grass
Seize my existence, bind
As in a prison, trees in mass.

And I in anchored space
Look to the sky to claim
More slopes and terraces.

Some so interior dwell
They need not penetrate
The close weather of their cell,

Or shut in dungeons hear
Voices; and from the dark
The brightest worlds draw near.

The Messenger

I don't deny that I believe in ghosts
Myself being one. No, not the ultimate last
Spirit, I mean, but this a messenger.
Soft, soft, last night half falling into sleep
I rose like smoke, up, curving past the window
Floating, a gray cloud seaward, slow and pale.

And then, the wings!

Did you hear the birds piling against your window?
A snow of wings, crowding and gentle, crying
Over and over, each with the single errand
Light cannot bring, nor ever my tongue would say.
Archaic doves, rustling your sleep, and calling
Crowding upon you, drifting and crying love.

Above the Earth

The mystical experience is love
Without an earthly object — one's slant of light
Or vivid emptiness; so I in this
Transported past proportion find my being.

And saints that capture heaven's flow
Rise on that stream beyond their narrow cells
Swung above earth, a silent choir
Being themselves a shrived and tenantless world

A god's breath. Who can hold
Such high hosanna through the sounding days?
But fall again to voice and restlessness
When the earth's shadow interrupts their flight,

And from such levitation dropping home
Cry out the luster of that glimpsed garden.

Pandora

Never, never again the house new or youth precise
Or the fresh loaves of hay in the field.
And the tree bark shimmers black and white
Only after rain.

The day rose clear-faced and quick
Breathing lemon and sage, undoubtedly crystal,
Fog was for coolness, not to get lost in, and the wicked
Rode to ominous music.

The box had been left, but I never suddenly opened the lid.
The day hung so full, time being happy and short,
No reason to fret over a dusty chest in a corner,
And I had given my word.

But nothing is changeless. While it was there in the house
Something crept out, buzzing and small.
I heard it at night, an insect whine in the air
Unseen in the light.

And the mornings were sad sometimes
And rising slow, and the day crumpled and worn
Like a picture handled too much,
And I indifferent.

Came haze outlasting the dawn
Between me and the fields, the horizon too close;
And bright days were full of objects
Not noticed before.

Love broke to a trinity, there were too many paths;
None seemed to be true, and in the oat fields the horsemen
Wore various guises, and which could I trust
On their spotted geldings?

I have heard of such things, but not for myself,
And the silver sifts from the box
On my hair and my tears, and the owner is gone, and I —
I shall never be rid of it.

The Protéstant

I never hold a thought
But what the opposite
Comes straightway into mind

Or cannot look at day
Except I see the night
Descending or ascend.

The place is, where we're bent
And ringing noon is high
Judged by an earthward slant.

Whatever I know I know
Only as April trees
Sucking the sap to green

Or as the simple seas
Answer a winter sound
Unstatable, unseen —

No sooner say I know
Than all my fibers turn
To prove it is not so.

To think God firm in heaven
Is to intenser learn
How shaken is that bough,

His good evades us still;
The solemn evidence
Proves death, dark, and evil.

As a lover or thrush
Embarrasses the hand —
Twice savory in the bush —

I pray and lie; I see
Spirit desired, denied
That when I come, I flee.

The Skyrocket

How sheer the arc I took, vagrant in speed,
Self-circling star, and breathed upon my flight,
Higher and slow and then again to height
Past summer bonfires, over the house the trees

Gathering suspense in the attempt to thrust
Beyond all earth! Then, sudden gasp and stop.
Elate, I puffed in fire and golden drops
Till the one brightness spread to nebulous.

And I, a single fleck, fall into dark
While strewn about, my sister selves, a shower
Of small and dimming lights, sift lower and lower
And pale and flake and disappear in calm.

The Sleeping Princess

I don't remember when I fell asleep,
Half up the stair, or dropped from a summer hill,
Or yawning into bedtime. But the dream
So counterfeited me, I could not tell

I was asleep. For in that sleep the sun
Shone on my eyes, I rose and breathed the day,
Widened the doors, ran to the summer lawn,
And spent the seasons prodigal as snow.

Still I was careful. There the sleeper lay.
I took such journeys as were possible.
My diary was complete, and it could show
Much was accomplished, and the days turned full.

And yet it was not real. I find the book
Dusty, unwritten in. For someone called
And touched my cheek. The spendthrift years were done.
Was it a kiss? I woke. And I was old.

Metamorphosis

Up from the earth in our spring
Grass ruffles the hills
And the wind catches
The yellow oriole's wing,
Snows petals under every plum.

On certain mornings from the range
Wind drags the valleys, trailing alpine cold
Toward rivieras turning on the sea,
Designs in apricot on southern walls.

If we should change
Is not this the season?
Rich branches push
Past frost and night
And the pliant fabrics rush
Toward the brown shapes of summer.

The Weathercock

Wind shakes me,
I am weak and spent
With every argument.
I doubt and hang
A breath disturbs me.
Sinewless and vain
The harsh and soft are one to me
Zephyr or gale, I turn my face to it.

North wind and south have whispered
And I go with each.
The dulcet evidence of bloom and spring
Or the cold reason of on-circling storm
Both have convinced me, and I yearn with them
Yearn as the smoke drift or the lifted leaves.

Yet I proportion my stance to the breeze.
Wind shall not take me
Though he shriek and bite
Frighten all other birds to leeward shade
Blow down the pigeons from the cooing lofts
Sail the hawk back downwind and send
Laborious eagles panting to their rocks.

I have set my claw
Deep in the roof's pinnacle,
There to hold
While solid objects knock about —
Each broadside thing —

Stiff in this hub to turn and, keen,
Broach to the wind a practiced waywarding.

Though the barn totters
And hay flies
And the wood is pierced by pebbles;
Till the ties of the timbers skew,
With the beams ajar,
And the shingles scatter
And the great roof falls

I crow though none may hear.
In the vast spinning world, I still point true.
I fly here.

The White Horse

Where is the white horse?
I asked the toyon and the walnuts.
The toyon was flowering,
The walnuts lifted their leaves lightly like feathers.
They were tossing and flowering and the wind rustled a little.
It was dark there under the trees.

I tried the meadow.
Where is the white horse
I asked the mustard and rye grass,
Have you seen her?
The mustard was yellow and the rye going to seed.
I could tell the old horse had been there.
She had left her mementos.

Where is the white horse?
I asked the towhees down by the corral.
They looked at me sideways.
One had already drowned in the water trough.
The birds had little to say. The corral was deserted.

I walked past the toyon and walnuts
And over the meadow and up the hill.
I knew the white horse had been there.
She's lame, I said, *she can't go far.*
And I went up the road to the next stable.
There was only a black horse and a brown one.

They tossed their manes on the wind and kicked their heels
        a little.

Where is the white horse, I said,
She was here yesterday.

Hidden Things

1

Upon the wall, drawn by a child's hand,
The horses twitch their tails or clash their hooves
In formal duel in an unreal land.
And they are sealed in stillness, though all moves

About them. No one sees them paw the air
For they are painted over, and no stain
Shows where they fly. Yet certainly they are there.
They are secret as the packet sealed with chain

To the courier's wrist, and even more, for none
Shall read what codes this flying herd might bring.
And so they stretch in their impenetrable zone.

2

Beneath engulfments of ocean, ground, and green

Between the lid of the box and the enclosed
Or the layers of paint or leaf, under sheared surfaces,
The hidden things broaden and are disposed
As rounded bodies in immeasurable space.

As gold beaten to foil may yet endure
Another stroke, and thin and thin again
So does each changing layer yield but more
The wheels and chambers of the finest plane.

No violence attains these inward stores.
Nor the slow fall of stealth, or shifts of day
Complete their rendezvous, although we shower
Echo with roar and labor. Suddenly

We are within the sound that we have made,
Within the box, and mystery surrounds
With vacancies of sun, enclosing shade
Of articulate blue. It is no simple ground

On which we walk, but treasuries of roots
And stones and hollow chambers, and the slow
Descent of parting things.   How lonely broods
The orchard, raising the green whispering show

Of summer through the roofs of cottages,
Through lawns and asphalt, in incorrigible tiers,
Remembered seasons, and beyond, in that place,
The waving grass of time's old furniture.

3

What lies beneath the terrace of flesh, the pale
Secluding forehead, in that weir of past
Illusions or hoped events? I cannot tell:
As one walks in darkness past a house

Suffused with radiance, and the curtains pulled
And curious, waits, discovers there a sum
Of uncovered light and finds within revealed
A shadow passing from the empty room.

But could I go within where dark and gold
Lean close together, hear the voices' tremor,

Still I would be outside each separate world
Illumined by its own conservator.

Alas, poor Psyche, did you think the fire,
The quick uncovering of the lamp would prove
By adding sight, the death of your desire?
You only changed unknown, for loss of, love.

4

Last night, happy and clear, I saw the dead.
We walked together over a wide lawn,
The living not more real than those dear shades,
And leaving to wake, I said farewell again.

Day world of birdsong, when I woke in light
And resonant morning, could any thought distress
This clear existence, paced by breath and bright
Air in which I move. For surfaces

Are hard, and depth the clean repeating of
The seen. The scene cut through and every leaf the same,
A chord of agate, into which we move,
The immortal hardening of a mortal plane.

Yet in this plain, by every light we sense
We lose as much, slipped back into that bend
Of suffering's waste, unrecollected suns —
Lose, and behold only the figured mind,

The dreamed, annihilable soul, psyche
Beyond the surface of the face, and there
Secretly rest. Where absolute abides
Abide all secret things, in an unbroken care.

The Walnuts

There shine always the bright tops of the grove
And within that forest mysteries of birds,
In the autumn, the clear crackle of leaves
And the walnut pickers. Dark-skirted after them

The gleaners. Trees, trees were everywhere.
Out of the banks of a foggy morning,
Outside the windows, the sweet trees leaned
Tasseled in spring, in holy burst of leaves.

And the oats made meadows of the early year —
With nodes for whistles, the juice sweet and thin —
Grown high to bend into rooms, and yellow flowers
Hung over the spicy tunnels under the trees.

There the grove, hanging forever real in the air.
And I an exile, knowing every turn
And turning home, and lost in the dazzled road
The strange, swept premises, and the great trees gone.

FROM

The Descent

1970

By the Woods, Reading

Something is creeping out between the words
The page dawdles its tune
While something slips up behind the wellpoint of the eye

Out there. And the highway roars past the pine trees
The firs that should never have grown there
In the first place. The trucks pass like waves
The old house shakes on their wheels.

But there is something drifting out of the sun
Not the weed puffs that glisten
Or the gnats, wing-caught by the sun.

It has been falling for weeks now.
The slow ash piles round my ankles
Rising from nothing but green —
Or I am sinking in a pond of dandelions.

It is winding between the trees
Tying them together. I am surrounded.
I walk into the dark eye.

Double Mirror

As this child rests upon my arm
So you encircled me from harm,
And you in turn were held by her
And she by her own comforter.

Enclosed, the double mirror runs
Backward and forward, fire to sun.
And as I watch you die, I hear
A child's farewell in my last ear.

Memorial

I will remember you into light
Or push by thinking into your quiet earth.
I will bring for you this hint of spring
I will think you a black twig with five white blossoms.
Heaven, earth, and man are on this branch.
I will will it to you through the dark
I will press it upon you, a talisman
For your eternity.
Voiceless, in silence, in darkness without sight
How will five blossoms thunder, how bright
Is this black bough, with nodes for shaking green,
Worlds to be born, and all creation burning
In this small bough brought backward into light.

In the Black Forest

Everywhere I go they are coming for me
In the shadow of night
Even through the trees of the Black Forest,
Flying, I suppose, over continents and oceans.

Everywere I go they find me
And drive up in the old car,
Stepping out, eager to embrace me.
We have not much to say to each other.

But how kind they are to come
Up out of my inner being,
Which they gave and which is really theirs —
And then back to the dark forest and the sea.

2

Gone, gone, but over me still
Broods the winged bird of their spirit
Made of their living breath.
It will last in their children forever.

It covers the bleak sky, a fierce mother —
And from the claws drift down ribbons
Curving scrolls with their mottoes
Which say *Do what you can* and *Take heart*.

The Fathers

I am beset by spirits, layer on layer
They hover over our sleep in the quilted air.
The owl calls and the spirits hang and listen.
Over our breaths, over our hearts they press.
They are wings and eyes, and they come surely to bless
There is hardly room for the crowd of them under the ceiling.

Remember me, remember me, they whisper.

The dark rustles, their faces all are dim.
They know me well, I represent them here.
I keep their lands, their gold and fruiting orchards,
I keep their books, their rings, their testaments.

I am their blood of life made visible
I hold their part of life that vanishes.
They whisper to me, names and messages,
Lost in the world, a sifting down of shadows.

I am myself, I say, it is my blood,
It is my time of sun and lifting of green,
Nothing is here, but what I touch and see.
They cry out *we are here in the root and tree.*
It is my night, I say — and yours for sleeping.
They move their wings, I think I hear them weeping.
Blest spirits, let me be.

Done With

My house is torn down —
Plaster sifting, the pillars broken,
Beams jagged, the wall crushed by the bulldozer.
The whole roof has fallen
On the hall and the kitchen
The bedrooms, the parlor.

They are trampling the garden —
My mother's lilac, my father's grapevine,
The freesias, the jonquils, the grasses.
Hot asphalt goes down
Over the torn stems, and hardens.

What will they do in springtime
Those bulbs and stems groping upward
That drown in earth under the paving,
Thick with sap, pale in the dark
As they try the unrolling of green.

May they double themselves
Pushing together up to the sunlight,
May they break through the seal stretched above them
Open and flower and cry we are living.

The Given Child

Most lost when found
Most found when lost.
We most must lose
When we love most.

1

In this season comes the child
Out of the black womb.
In this season
Comes the risen god.
In this season
You are born.
In this season lost too.

The sun ranges to the dangerous south
The shortening days speak night to us.
On the turning sun
You enter.

The sun spins in darkness where you grow
Unheeding our voices.

Become in this season yourself.
You do not need us,
Carried in the dark like the sun
To enter and grow like summer.

2

We gave you life
And that is the great treasure
And now my blood goes circling in the world
I do not know your name.
Henceforth I love all strangers, loving you.
In their young eyes
I see my own reflection.

Unknown child
What was the best?
You take my unpossessing
Everywhere
In a great round of blood, guilt, love.

3

This is the place where there were fields and marshes
And the red-winged blackbirds flew
Up from the rushes.
Olive orchards older than remembering
Covered the hills
And beyond, the orange groves
Dead now, unnatural, bare of leaves.

This cross road I never saw before.

But the hills with the oil wells are the same
Black derricks — and the walking beams
Chug up and down
Where the yellow violets grew in spring.

The jack-rabbit road is straight now
And the trees by my mother's house
Are gone
And the house too and the pond.

4

We shall leave our bones on the mountain

While it rains, try to find shelter.
If the sun shines, get out of the shadow.
Dry off if you can.
Try to keep going.
If you find berries
The birds have left
Nibble them first.
Grasses are all right to chew.
Be careful of nightshade.

Look for a stream.
Go down beside it.
It will be hard to follow
But if anyone is near at all
They will live by the stream or a bridge will cross it.
Find a road and you may find a cabin.
If they are not there, break in.

It is a long way down.
Don't push too hard.
The bushes will tear at you.

It will be cold where you go.
It will be cold here on the mountain.

Letter from Portugal

For Barbara — An Elegy

I have come a long way from my country
To find it once more in the clusters of purple
Bougainvillea, hibiscus, the red oleander.
Here grapes too and olives
And oaks on the brown hills.

Autumn in my country, autumn in Portugal
The grapes are purple and red, black are the shadows,
Dry leaves, and the wind blows into the belvederes.
Wind flicks the dry fields over the slopes of the hills
Presses up the undersilver of leaves.

At night the wind brings sounds of children calling
Across the blue cleavings of the sea
Calling *come home, come home.*

— And you in that dark country where you walk
In a dry season, without fountains,
In the color of shade, the rich host of purple
With weighted head by the still river wandering
In that sleeping country,

That was the country that was always yours
To which you always went at evening —
Dark and cool as the shallows of these gardens —
Lost now and listless in the windless darkness
Under the deep pennons of the trees.

Under broad calm, across dull undersea
The children weep. Do you not hear them call —
And move and stir under the heavy shadow —
Come back to us, o prodigal.

The Flood

When I sat beside the river
Thinking of waves higher than buildings
Waves descending like barges down the smooth channel
I thought I dreamed.

But the water came high —
It filled the cellar
Covered grandmother's canned pears
And the quilts by the fireplace.

It rose above grandfather's portrait
Lapped at our feet on the second story.
We looked down the stairs.
Would the house hold?

Could we float on that Ark
Through the corn fields
Downtown past the first national bank
And Gluth's grocery store?

Logs and fence posts piled up by the house.
The pigs flowed away, complaining.
Night was coming down,
The waters pushed at the foundations,
Our dog whined in the upstairs bedroom.

What could we do but sit there?
We made a raft of the bedstead
And a plank off the bedroom dresser.

We were ready to knock a hole in the wall
For launching. But the stream began to go down.

It went down to mud. The crops were gone,
The animals lost or dead. But we were alive.
The old house as good a ship as any.
Whenever I look at the river
I think of those waves and wonder.

Night Rain

I wake with the rain.
It has surprised me.
First, delight,
Then I think of outdoors:
The shovels and rakes I left in the garden
Rusting now in the mist,
The splintering of handles.
I think of car windows open
Tricycles
Canvas cots, trash cans
The hay uncovered
Mildew.

Well, they are out.
And the animals —
The cat, he is gone
The dog is the neighbor's
The horses have a tin roof
If they will stay under it.
And the wild things are there —
Birds, wet in the trees,
Deer in the brush, rabbits in hiding.
The leaves will all be washed
The wild lilacs, the walnuts.

I am sleepy and warm
I dream of the great hornéd owl
Snatching birds like plums out of trees.

The Beating

The first blow caught me sideways, my jaw
Shifted. The second beat my skull against my
Brain. I raised my arm against the third.
Downward my wrist fell crooked. But the sliding

Flood of sense across the ribs caught in
My lungs. I fell for a long time,
One knee bending. The fourth blow balanced me.
I doubled at the kick against my belly.

The fifth was light. I hardly felt the
Sting. And down, breaking against my side, my
Thighs, my head. My eyes burst closed, my
Mouth the thick blood curds moved through. There

Were no more lights. I was flying. The
Wind, the place I lay, the silence.
My call came to a groan. Hands touched
My wrist. Disappeared. Something fell over me.

Now this white room tortures my eye.
The bed too soft to hold my breath,
Slung in plaster, caged in wood.
Shapes surround me.

No blow! No blow!
They only ask the thing I turn
Inside the black ball of my mind,
The one white thought.

On the Way

The day after Christmas. Everything is clean
And bright by rains, the leaves on the acacias
And toyon. Stopped up the hill I can see

The mountains, gray with gashes of snow
And the ocean glaring in the sun.
I could see boats if there were any.

But the sea is a clear table top.
I go down the hill. Things glisten. The clouds
Are clean-edged on painted blue.

Down by the boulevard the palm trees
Are having their fronds cut. They drop
From the heads of the stolid date palms

And the thin cocos a hundred feet high.
A man in a crow's nest on top of a crane
On top of a truck is doing the job.

Fronds fall, missing the man in the turtle-neck
Sweater and the woman in the leopard coat
Who wait for the bus. Roses — notice: don't pick — bloom in
    the park.

I pass Gogian's Tire Honesty and the tracks
Where I have never seen a train. Fat pigeons
Are grazing on the grass between the ties.

Three men are coming home from the moon.
Carloads of skiers go off to the mountains.
This hour's all I count on.

The Committee

Black and serious, they are dropping down one by one to the
    top of the walnut tree.
It is spring and the bare branches are right for a conversation.
The sap has not risen yet, but those branches will always be bare
Up there, crooked with ebbed life lost now, like a legal
    argument.
They shift a bit as they settle into place.
Once in a while one says something, but the answer is always
    the same,
The question is too — it is all *caw* and *caw*.
Do they think they are hidden by the green leaves partway up
    the branches?
Do they like it up there cocking their heads in the fresh
    morning?
One by one they fly off as if to other appointments.
Whatever they did, it must be done all over again.

from AN AMERICAN GALLERY

Dolly Hazlewood

Untitled
oil, c. 1940

The peach orchard faces the woods
And in between
Runs a narrow of bluebonnets.

The peach trees slant down a hill
Pungent with bloom
And are caught against a rock wall.

The wall is the only sign of man
And it seems fallen.
The picture is a celebration of spring

In which between the woods and the orchard
Bluebonnets cover the earth
And tint every hill under the sky.

Could the artist be saying that man's
Works are succumbing to nature?
Or that in between

Nature and art is the place for bluebonnets?
Or did she on that heart-full morning
Simply frame the best view of her flowers?

Great Aunt Doll was a woman of spirit.
When she died at last in a sanitarium
She was making a vast collection of seashells.

Philip Evergood

American Tragedy
oil on canvas, 1937

South of Chicago, the black chimneys of the steel mills
are soiling the sky. Their walls are red. No one is near them.
But there is action aplenty. A corps of policemen
armed with night-sticks and guns
are beating the fleeing citizens.

The night-sticks are raised and fall with equal pity
on men and women, fair-skinned and dark.
They rain on the shirt-sleeved men and the women in
      summer dresses.
A man falls backward, his chin thrown up by a fist.
An Italian clutches his chest where a bullet has found him.

Those who can are running away.
A black man lies on his face, blood falls from his mouth.
He holds in his hand the flag of the land of the free.
None shall escape, the policemen work hard.
They are shooting the blonde woman in the pink dress

While she, her hands empty, held high, runs from
that blue army. In the center a man holds back the police
      with his hand,
his arm is around the Mexican woman in green.
Her fist is clenched, she holds a stick as weapon.
She is pregnant. A club hangs over this man's head.

The red of the wall of the mill colors the scene.
It drips from the brow of the man who has lost his straw hat,
from the mouth of the black man, from the chest of the other.
It will break from the heads of the red-headed man
And the woman in green. Puddles, bright as blood
Or the melting pots of the mills, color the streets of the city.

Edward Hicks

The Peaceable Kingdom
oil on wood, c. 1830

This was the peaceable kingdom: the river flows
like time beside it. This tiny slope,
grass covered, slants up to an impassable forest.

Half up the sky a natural bridge
curves like a rainbow. In such a place
Penn pledged his peace to all his Indian brothers.

He stands there, engraved, given to fat,
his friendly hands extended to the natives
who, lean as Caesar, accept his fatal gifts.

But that good Quaker in his peaceful country
is past and backdrop. On this crowded shore
herded together, the wolf and the lamb lie down

And the tiger looks at the kid as once
in the garden of Eden, innocent of blood.
The calf, the young lion, the fatling lie together.

And the cow and the bear share their ration of straw,
the lion and the ox beside one another, surprised.
The eagle and dove eat from the hands of a child.

Another plays with the serpent. In all this mountain
there is no danger, for the earth is filled
with the word of the lord. There is no hunger.

How could this be? Even here, withdrawn on a mountain,
where the quail and dove walk at the grasses' edges,
I hear the world washing away my kingdom.
The deer go by, seeking the last wild ranges.

On the Death of the President

November 22, 1963

In a current of eagles and parks and green,
In a blue ripple of shouts, in the hearty sun,
The day moves with autumn and feasting,
Cheers, and the rustle of crowds, and the held faces.

Stretched beyond the green savannahs of our knowing
Deep in marshes and trees, in scrub oak, the deer
Stands flicking his shoulders, dappled in shade.
The dogs scare up the autumn colors of partridge.

The world centers on noon, the White Mountains have
     passed it,
The Rockies still hold morning's sun on the early snow.
In the Cascades the spruces cast their shadows westward.
The country gathers toward noon in the midst of the country.

Into the forest of our knowing, across the marked paths,
Over the billow of flags and the hails and the shot,
Beneath the crowd's crumpled breath,
Hunted and fallen, the fated and noontime meet.

Noon turns suddenly black, and the sigh falls over
The sun like the shadow of all the mists of breath,
Like a prayer tears fall among the avenues,
The noon's huge sun wrapped in the mists of mourning.

Through the long afternoon a coffin rides the skies
Death flies above, the air weeps at his passing,

Awake we dream out woe, the day curves on,
Earthbound, we walk through autumn bells and harvests.

In afternoon's fields we gather, we gather in folds
And all the flowers are garnered and gathered
In the mountains, in the fields and towns, under the pine trees:
Goldenrod, firethorn, buckwheat, red-leaved sumac.

Into the soft-leaved evening we wait and the flight is ended.
End and beginning and end, forever and ever.
The dead and the living
Enter the darkening field — and each to his fortune.

While the dark with its loss falls over the capital
And seeps over the Potomac into the fields of Arlington
And spreads over West Virginia and the Appalachians
And drops over the great plains of the Mississippi
Engulfs the Bad Lands and the Black Hills
And creeps slowly up over Sante Fé and the Sangre de Cristo
Over the Wind River and the Great Basin and the Mojave
And high, high over the Sierra Nevada — without a star —
And drifts down over the calm Pacific.

The Speed of Planes

They have been falling from the sky
Ever since they went there
And the two wings, upper and lower,
Were stretched, catching the wind
Straining upward, a kite
To the sun. The wings have changed us.

> Noisy and hurrying we forget
> To listen, we forget the wind
> That once said winter is coming,
> We forget the walking on the earth,
> We forget the midnight message
> And the slow drifting of small things.

Till in the offering of fire
We have poured our children.
We heard them laughing together
While the planes hurled overhead.
We heard all turn to silence
In the building of the flame.

The Descent

Let us, therefore, bend all our force and
thoughts of soul to this most holy light,
that showeth us the way which leadeth to
heaven; and after it, putting off the affec-
tions we were clad withal at our coming
down, let us clime up the stairs which at
the lowermost step have the shadow of
sensual beauty, to the high mansion-place
where the heavenly, amiable, and right
beauty dwelleth.

BALDASSARE CASTIGLIONE

As I descend from ideal to actual touch
As I trade all the golden angel crowns
And rings of light for gross engrossing sense,
As I descend Plotinus's stairs,
Angel, man, beast, but not yet plant and stone,
The sense of that height clings, the earthen hand

Transmutes again to light, is blessed from black
Through alchemy to rise rich red, green, blue,
Fractions of vision broke from ample crowns.

As I from the mind's distance fall on voyages
I test the strength of water where I walk
And lose the air for wings. I am lifted
As I descend past clouds and gusts of air
As I go down with wind to tops of trees
As I walk down from mountain tops and cold.

As I descend to gardens warm with leaves
As I enter the new morning harsh in sun
I count the earth with all its destinies
Come down to prove what idea does not know.

I descended out of nothing into green
I descended out of spaces where the spare
Stepping stones of islands roughed my way.
I descended into solidness, to dense
And mingled shrubberies where the birds
Alone choose wings for crossing my old sky.

Caught in this day within a sound of hours
Walled into shadows, stripped of multitudes,
I try this spring the growing into light.

In the Husk

In the darkness of this womb
Or this winding
Done up in cords spun
Out of myself
I wait.

There was light
And I consumed
Husks, leaves, veins
Drinking the sap
Turning the long pith
Into silk
That now enfolds me.

It is at last this darkness
That I have come to
Tired of moving about
Of lifting the head
And the searching feet
Set carefully among the branches.

I am shaken down
Falling into my silken dream.

O this dark dark winding into the dark
Immobile, insignificant
Self-tied, self-prisoner
Not dead, not living, but moving on
To the new air I have not yet conceived.

The Organization of Space

1

Vacancy goes with me as does a sea,
Perfect, round, in all directions sending
All the not-where, where that one is not bending,

Or the wide disk of grain, shadeless of trees,
Empty, and the arch empty, of seeing,
Above, below, unconscious of that being,

And the great desert parched of all —
No rock, no shadow — without green or air —
Only salt and dry, that center being not there.

2

Add to the dull disk of sea, colors of coral,
A speck of land within brief shafts of water —
Then we have distance and before and after.

Set in the midst of grain a single tree
And like a magnet pulling into place,
It draws a path across the unlined space.

And in the desert the uprising stone
Cuts into space and makes the skies convene.
Landmarks arise, and in the shade a green.

3

I praise a local vista, clipped or rough.
It makes its variants with sun and frost —
Hill, row, and field — till vacantness is lost.

And from such centering, the wires that join
The farm and town, the seen and unseen line
Can mark out waves' and gravity's design.

Arched like a row of tents with canvas seams,
The sky is propped by pole and spire to show
They hold the circles fixed through which I go.

4

And yet a vacancy, an almost none,
An arching of the mind into a sky
Under which empty fields and barrens lie,

A round of almost gone, a black and sere,
Returns across the vivid local tiers
And turns them to a round, unshaded sea.

Spirit or being, corn-god or harvester,
That sets us deep within the year's concern,
Hold the circumference in which we turn.

In the Lenten Season

Risen, the masquerade of flesh
Compounds this floating spring, the plane
Of trees, bloom, terrace, where we pass
The garrulous afternoon. The noun

Is what is feared: to name the sly
Commotion of the blood which runs
Unplanned as leaves to their own ways.
The day ends in a double vision

Of the self immaculate, and its brood
Of interior dwellers — kernel and shell:
The token ritual, grown hard,
And the sweet corruptible.

The Late Visitor

Listen, let me explain, it was not the fire
That burned in the hearth and kept me there.
It was no real fire, though I swear it did seem so
And to go out was to step into blackest snow,
And to stay was to lose, not find. Words only say
What is gone. Or are motions like flame and snow,
Slow circlings of something about to occur,
The birth of a salamander in the fire.

I am caught between never and now. You must tell me to go.

The Gift

It was round, orb being most nearly perfect,
And warm perhaps, though hardly of any color,
Smelling of spring, faintly, of hyacinth.
It was not fruit, though on those trees first planted
Eastward, of life and knowledge, it may have grown.
There were many trees in Eden. And this not eaten.
Yet flower neither, though soft as petals
Yet harder perhaps, like pearls hunted
Through dark shore-caves, or rubies hidden,
Precious as those, glanced at and not seen.
Transparent, then, and gone like water
Floating off, yet here; and single, out of many,
And not illusion, though it may have been.
Solid and constant, ephemeral and shaken,
Fruit, flower, or stone, or given or taken.

Morning

From the center of our body
Come the bright flowers.

Draw open the curtain
And we shall see them
On bush and stone.

Let us exchange our borders
That I may speak with your voice.

Mirror

In this mirror your face is broken
The sockets of your eyes
Cleave from the cheeks
And the smile pulls
Half a face.
There is a wen behind your ear
And the knuckles of your hands
Grow large.
Your skin is withered.
Your hand shakes.
I loved you.
I am lost.

A Birthday

On the morning of my birthday I awoke from a dream
Where I came down from walking in a park on a hill.
The hill had two sides: on one the bright chaparral
Stood separate and shining on the brown hay of summer
On the other, pineshade — and ferns on the floor of a forest.
They vanish away as smoke in the air.

The ground was soft underfoot
It was evenly planted; all things were in order.
I was barefoot, and it was holiday
And I came down and found the streets full of people
And I walked in full and swinging skirts among them.
He is great that sets at nought all worldly honor.

Beloved, we go west to the wide sea
All of us, coming down from the hill.
All of us, all, borne on the shell of earth —
Though far from the sea you ride.
And I may behold all things as they be, of short abiding.

At my center is a pool, calm
Dark. I have not found its edges.
And as I turn westward
Though I have not found wisdom
The great pool of peace is the center, what I am and that only.
May nothing take from thee inward liberty of soul.

In this first morning of my year I awoke
And all things were hung with light.

Night of Souls

I saw each soul as light, each single body
With his life's breath kindled and set like flame
Before his nostrils. All creatures visible —
Small beings moving in the midnight grasses,

Light in the thoroughfares underfoot
The mole's house hung with the mole's breath
As with candles, and the busy air
Clouded with light.

It is no longer midnight, for the sea
Rustles translucent waters, windows letting out
The glow of all its denizens, colored as through
Cathedral glass, the night sky dark
Save where a lost gull drops like a meteor
Into the phosphorous waves.

The linnets chirp as in daylight. The owl dazzles himself.
Silent and still, wondering by the glare of his mother
The new colt shines.
Light betrays the young deer in the thicket

On this night of the lighting of spirits
All quiet, all visible
Till the lantern of man comes up over the hill,
Shades out those other beams like a bare sun rising.

Numbers

When we think of numbers, they are what move
In the wind, over the ground, through the thick seines
Of water. Small. They rustle around us.

Or silent. What can't be counted. I have seen
A hive of bees hang on a branch of our lilac
The wild thorny blue of the endless blossoms.

Now in autumn here the leaves turn from numbers
Become mass where the wild walnuts
Plan now the deluge of spring from the ends

Of the dying branches. And the meek, and grass,
Move toward inheritance. New fish in the streams.
I have dreams beyond count and remember.

Going Away

The horses are going away
The tall mare and the four-year-old.
Their bridles lie by the drive,
And their gear and what is left of the oats.

They do not know. They are out there sleeping.
Over them the tin roof bangs in the wind.

They will wade into acres of grass
And hear the new sound of a sea
That breaks past the hill and the steady branches of oaks
In a place where the roads have not come yet.

How they will run in the big pasture
Or stand, flicking their tails in the sunlight
Those high beasts that looked over our shoulders
Or stood silent, nuzzling, blocking the way.

They called to us when we were slow at evening.
The young one was born here.

We will go back into our houses
We will forget how large the world was once.

To Her Spirit at the Winter Solstice

Now the year ends darkly.
The sun drifts in the south.
Will it ever return?

And you force me in the cold to gather red berries
Up early in mist, breaking the branches —
The musky smell of the toyon —
Will this be enough?

Look down, spirit, from your height of fire,
Look from the skiff crossing the black river.
Call back the sun that lingers.

Shall I bring only remembering
Who cannot bring flowers? for the cold
Grows deep and dark where you linger.

And the ship of fire goes farther
Toward some chill cape of waves and darkness.
Hold fast in the rough riding.

O blown spirit, do not draw me
To those chill tides
Where I too cast my offerings
In darkness.

Weeds

Nothing so startles us as tumbleweeds in December
Rising like ghosts before us in the headlamps
The big round weeds blowing into fences
Into guard rails and wheels, wedged into corners
Drifting in ranks over roads in a gusty order
Round in the orbits of winter, dropping the invisible seed,
Blown green and purple-leaved into springtime, soft with water,
Filled to harsh circles in the thirsty summer
Dried brown and jagged, ready for December
When the silver globes, magnificent in procession
Slow and solemn-paced in the ritual of ending
Dry, dead, in the dim-most part of the year
Spread the great round promises of green morning.

FROM

In Mediterranean Air

1977

Glimmerglass

This lake is the center of the story.
All that happens the lake makes possible.
This lake has deeps for graves and shoals for building.

On a shoal in the lake there is a fortress
A house that resembles a ship, round which the tides
Drift in predictable fashion, like a cradle rocking.

All is at hand, lake trout rise to the hook
Deer come down to drink, easy for taking,
Ducks and geese by the bagful. Berries grow on the shore.

What a monotony of noble days and nights!
The cliffs softened by trees, the water birds calling
The lake glimmering as sun and stars take turns above it.

Outside the ring — the house, the lake, the shore —
The unbroken forest. There the enemy waits
Circling and stalking the house in the center.

Round within round to the very eye
That watches from the knothole, the heart that hides
In the house in the lake in the circle of the forest.

Dreaming of Foxes

Dreaming of foxes
coyotes and the deer
that used to hang about the garden
nuzzling the fresh green
their breaths smelling of roses

I was tempted to wake
but saying, no, into
this dream I will dissolve
I will go
down into its well of water.

What will I find there
that the morning birds
will not carry away
those lakes of blue, teeming,
by snowy mountains.

Out of the mountains
came the birds in line
took the pieces of my dream
the shreds of lake water
threaded them among the trees
in the leaves where they sit waking.

I Thought Back and

There I was
at the top of the walnut tree
in my old red sweater
my dress catching on twigs
my legs scratched from climbing.
Wind bent the boughs
almost to breaking:

> Growing in every cell
> I never once thought of you
> thinking about me.

> Your problem is forever looking
> backward.
> All you see is me
> waiting for the next big
> noisy gust of wind
> to hang from.

> All you see is me
> not thinking of you,
> old woman,
> me singing.

One April

When I go away, this will become a picture
the big river flowing deep and still past the front door
the poinciana about to burst with red flowers
a few mosquitoes buzzing, but not yet many,
and the air heavy by the palmetto thicket.

Things are going to stay this way for a long time.
Whatever I do, my uncle is going to be here
smoking his cigarette, talking of shorthorn cattle
and Doll, the gardener, with his shears
will be snipping a mound of foliage early in the morning
while Esther stirs in the kitchen among pancakes.

I am leaving now, but the scene will never change.
If I come back, things will start again.

Our Town

This is the village where we grew
Our fathers and their sires in line
The trees they planted shade the view
And the white houses shine.

The families here had come to stay
The preacher was the parson's son
And if one brother moved away
We kept the solid one.

We tended order in the town
Our lawns were trim, our hedges green
And in the countryside around
The furrows straight and clean.

We went to church, obeyed the laws
And voted on election day.
The peaceful farms surrounded us
The battles always far away.

And when the soldiers came to town
With drums and our flag overhead,
We watched them from the commons lawn
Until they shot us dead.

Libraries

Always being burned by vandals
of whatever name
next to the temple
papyri
browned, curled, the paint flaked off
the secrets of the gods
a black smoke only.

Or breaking through the ill-kept door —
the scriptorium littered with fallen flowers
the acanthus scattered among vowels
the blossoms not of this world, the enameled petals
gilt stems falling underfoot, saints
and the pointed hills crowding the margins,
the prayers divided, the visions gobbed in blood
the girt-robed guards dead or leaving.

And the pyres at the street corner
added to page by page
smoldering among the righteous.

The secrets coded, the hillside with its kings
stares down at us, the undecipherable,
the tablet that means victory. Whose? When?
The clay messages wash down to pebble
the scroll torn, packing for urns
  fair face   *engrained*
is all it tells us.

Water, fire, enemy bombardment
the careless sky, the slow damp of nightfall
the gathering and division
Khufu, Thebes, Alexandria
Rome, Monte Cassino.

Leather reeks an invitation.
I sit by the wall
of a deep well
while the slow fire of hours
darkens the pages.

Prophet

In the fifteenth year of the emperor Tiberius
he hunted hives of wild bees
breaking open the hollows of wood or bone
seizing the sweet marrow.
Quicker than grasshoppers
he crunched wing and belly.
His face gnarled under the sun.
At night he crawled under
a goatskin. The air was thin out there
the stars big as melons.
The brook for water or washing in
or to cleanse an occasional stranger of his wickedness.
His hair matted. His dry beard
bristled away from his jaw.
Ravens flew by sometimes. Small groups of men
he shouted to, came, bringing others.
Clearly the world couldn't go on like this.

The Four Horsemen

In our country the hills lie like tawny lions
green in spring, turning yellow with summer
here and there oak trees, with cattle under them
and in the broadest valleys, villages.

If strangers come along, we notice them.
Like those four, resting their horses
by the small stream there, under the oak tree.

Riders, and even from the distance
I can tell their horses are splendid, well-fed
faster than ours, and their trappings expensive.

Even from here they seem unusual travelers.
There's the one with the sorrel, a heavy man
black-bearded, restless, he aims his gun
at every bird, as if eager for hunting.

The thin one can't stand still either.
He is picking the stalks that grow around him
stripping the oats off, twisting the hollow stems
into knots and whistles. His horse is the black stallion.

And the plump palomino, stomping to be off
belongs to the man in the pale overcoat
who remains stock still, as if content where they are.

The fourth, in the yellow Stetson, waits apart from the others.
Whether he is their friend or enemy is hard to say.
Have they come for a duel in this deserted pasture?

I would go close if I dared, either to welcome them
to the village or find out their business.
But there is something so strange in their manner —

the oats falling back in a circle around them, the ground
growing dark, a cloud breaking the sun's warmth.
Better go back to town and see what's doing.

Those four may mean no harm, but no good certainly.
And I keep thinking of the balance of things
and how we might change should they settle among us.

Mr. D

I think of you sometimes, how you came.
You were in brown, a patterned garment,
putting your hand on my forehead — yes
it was hot — and my tongue

was loose in my mouth, my eyes rattled
in sockets grown too large. Each part
of myself departed from every other.
I was a grand central station of departures

a kind of wormy seedbed, like your coat
a patchwork. Baling wire was what I needed
to keep the straws of me all together.
I didn't care much. And you were gentle.

You softened the pillow where my head sank
into a swamp. You helped me settle
my parts on the raft I was floating off on.
I slept easy knowing you were there.

You told me how to dream without dreaming
like the roots under the snow in winter.
Dark, and knowing that darkness, warm
and held like a comfort around me.

Heat Wave

has blasted the vines
their leaves fold up to the veins
like torn umbrellas. Fruit bakes in light
birds hide by the trunks of trees.
The earth is about to become a sun.
Yellow clouds of smoke and fog
embrace the sky. The day itself a fire
we are too close to.
Roses open dry petals, holly like buckshot
buckthorn, slick rhus, even the walnuts
clutch useless leaves. Ivy goes brown in the scab of weeds.
Fire is coming on the hot wind.
Here and there it will clean up the earth
heavy with old debris.

Holding Our Own

A summer without passion
our selves pulled together
like the leaves surrounding the branches
each branch part of the tree
the tree round, holding its own in the air.

The music begins
round globes of sound
weld it together
it balloons in the night
circles the amphitheater
whole and separate
as the star that winks at the proceeding.

And we in our own atmosphere —
the bear in the globe
of a child's toy
shaken, a blizzard
encloses him
inside the water in the ball.

Each walking in our round of air
through the long summer
without anger, without joy, with no surprise.
Now in August the leaves begin to turn
walnuts — black globes — rattle the eaves.

When the leaves burn to yellow
and brambles conquer the garden

one day comes a clear draft from the north
and the sky goes blue once more.

We smell the cool pain of autumn
in the green chemical light
waiting for waking
to shake us — birds in the cat's mouth —
or fall back numb again
among the chill, murdered, murdering leaves.

THE WOMEN OF PERSEUS

Danae

I am caught here
in the held air
while outside the day
moves in the leaves.

Voices ripple
from far away,
the road disappears
in the dusty wind.

My blood sounds in my ears
like a river of brass
and the hills at the sky line
turn bronze with blossoms.

My thoughts wither
and vanish in circles where I imagine
down by the stream the footpath
crowded with passers.

Unreal from this distance
the processions as on a vase
the lovers leaning on one another
the world going about its business.

And my life here
an echoing bell

calling me nowhere,
the days rising and falling like wheatfields.

2

Night is my own.
The tower a shadow in shadows.
Down its sides run
ladders of leaves

shining vines and tendrils
stairways of broken mirrors
the rivers flash by
dreaming.

And the fish in their shifting schools
catch the light
like a secret.

Birds drowse in the trees
and the light lies over the white fields,
all taut, sheer surfaces,
that resound for a moment
the echo of light.

3

The days go by in gold
lazy and bright
warm in reflection
where waves shallow up yellow sands.

I catch light in my arms.
Dust powders the air

and the motes
spatter its rays in blinding echoes.

Soft as the chaff
that drifts from the winnowed grain
the sun heaps down on me
covers me in drifts

and the warm waves harden
into sinews of bronze.
Radiant with sun
my lover presses upon me.

4

First my father set me in this tower
among tripods burning with incense,
pampered with waiting women, fed on dishes of gold,
my garments bordered in purple, my arms
circled by amulets rich with jewels.

My handmaidens laugh, weaving endless garlands of flowers
        and green.
The tower is fragrant and airy, and I can see far into distance.

I would rather live in a cottage by the rough waves,
the wife of a fisherman, waiting at evening for the day's
        small catch
or in the hut of a ploughman in a stone-blunted upland.

The old man my father most of all fears time,
the grey already creeps in his beard and his hair,
jealous that his child grows beautiful beside him,

fears his own seed, knowing he will go down,
his strength stolen nightly, rising in his children.

I have lain with the sun, my lover,
and the sun's child will burst forth from my dark
at morning.

5

It is dark as the underworld here and when I try
to lift my head I strike the rough top
of the chest that they put me in. I still hear echoes of blows
on the top hammering home, splinters torture my fingers
where I struggled against the wood. I cannot see
to ease them out. My head aches from striking
the lid of the chest. I cannot raise my knees.
I screamed but heard no one. They worked in silence.

Now beaten by waves the box lurches and turns
rolling me here and there. The holes left for air
take in water. Already it sloshes
around me. I am cold, and the child with me
cries. The air reeks of him. He searches
with puny hands for my breast. His mouth
blind in the dark plucks at me. I am thirsty.
My father had been kinder to kill me outright
with a clean stroke. I am sick
with tossing. The box closes in, the water rises.
They have left me no means to destroy myself.

Starve, drown, suffocate.
These are my gifts
from my father who starved me of love

from my lover who drowned me in love
from my son for whose birth I die in this stinking box.
Zeus, who descended in sunlight
if once I shone in your favor
when your bright form grew in sudden rays
      remember your son.

    6

Now I live in the fisherman's cottage I once longed for.
The sea snarls over rocks, my son goes out with the fishers
or runs with the herdsmen's sons.
I wear the brown dress of the poor.

There is always something to do.
Water must be brought from the well
goats must be milked, cheese made, figs picked and dried,
olives pressed, and the eternal spinning.

The island is small and poor
the king's palace a house like the others.
Goats graze right up to the doorposts.
His brother is a fisherman.

They have given me a clumsy girl as a serving-maid
and the king looks my way too often.
The beauty that brought a god from heaven
withers in this forsaken island.

The Graeae

We were always old, always turning away
from ripeness, without ever knowing springtime,
our hair hung in wrinkled strands
and no one ever looked at us.

We were born on a coast covered with grey clouds
all day. We have been here forever.
Grey sedge, grey rocks stretched up from dirty sand
a beach littered with weed and cast up timbers.

Nothing ever prospered here, the bushes covered with spines
a few water birds lost and quickly leaving
or adding a flat carcass to the draggled strand.
We had few hopes and nothing came of any.

Bit by bit we lost what little we had —
our teeth, our eyes, the rhythm of walking.
From the beginning the flat shore closed us in.
Three cold grey stones we sit here doing nothing.

Medusa

Had I but known when I saw the god approaching!
His horses pulled him briskly over the water
as on dry land, wreathed in seaweed, dripping,
his chariot shone gold in the warm summer.
I stood as he walked — the old man — up from the shore.
He climbed the temple stairs. He praised my grace.
I had never seen a god before.
He seized and raped me before Athena's altar.

It is no great thing to a god. For me it was anger —
no consent on my part, no wooing, all harsh
rough as a field hand. I didn't like it.
My hair coiled in fury; my mind held hate alone.
I thought of revenge, began to live on it.
My hair turned to serpents, my eyes saw the world in stone.

2

Whatever I looked at became wasteland.
The olive trees on the hill as I walked down
rattled in wind, then stood — as if a hand
had fashioned them of bronze. I saw the town
where I was raised become a stone. The boys
ran by as on a frieze, the charioteer
whipping his horses, held his arm, mid-air.

His horses stopped in stride. My hair
started to hiss. I hurried to my door.

The servant with his water jar upraised
stands there forever. I strode across the floor.
My furious glance destroyed all live things there.
I was alone. I am alone. My ways
divide me from the world, imprison me in a stare.

3

The prisoner of myself, I long to lose
the serpent hair, the baleful eyes, the face
twisted by fury that I did not choose.
I'd like to wake up in another place,
look for my self again, but there recur
thoughts of the god and his misdeed always —
the iron arm, the fall, the marble floor
the stinking breath, the sweaty weight, the pain,
the quickening thrust.

                    And now the start,
the rude circling blood-tide not my own
that squirms and writhes, steals from me bone by bone —
his monster seed growing beneath my heart,
prisoned within my prison, left alone,
despised, uncalled for, turning my blood to stone.

Andromeda

I am terrified
marooned on a rock with a gale
freshening and the waves already
spatter me with spindrift.

What could my father be thinking of!
Listening to a two-faced oracle,
chaining me like a dog in this gnashing water.
It is low tide now — high tide will be the end of me.

I will either drown struggling against water
or be caught here by the monster from the sea
the claws searing me along the bone
the teeth quick cutting through flesh and nerve.

It is grim being a sacrifice.
The garlands, the watching crowds, cannot make me heroic.
My legs tremble and fire streaks across my brain
the roots of my hair are daggers.

If this were a story there would be a hero
to swim through the impossible waves, a sword at his belt.
He would cast off my chains, kill the monster, take me
out of this country mad with fear and riddles.

But all I am sure of is the explosion of waves,
my mother crying from the shore, the seething wings
of a large invisible bird circling the rock,
and the head of the monster coming up over the horizon.

Perseus

Because my mother mated with a god
I am by birthright a hero.
This brings responsibility. I have had to excel at games —
running, wrestling, throwing the spear and the discus,
and to undertake long journeys at a moment's notice.

My mother, being alone, brought me up as best she could
and I have always deferred to her wishes.
I have had to keep her unwanted lover at bay
and, as he was king, conciliate him too.
That is how I encountered my first adventure.

Bring back the head of Medusa, he told me
as if it were easy. Being young, I agreed.
I didn't even know where to find her, but I had help
from my brothers and sisters, the eternal gods.

They equipped me with wings, a shield, a sickle, and a cap
         of darkness
and pointed west. I flew up, high over the island
and saw how small it was. I flew on over the sea
until toward sunset I found the three old women.

They sat there, hardly moving, toothless and blind —
at least only one tooth and one eye among them,
which they passed round. I felt sorry for them
but I took the eye and the tooth anyway
and they pointed out Medusa.

She was asleep. Maybe she had once been beautiful
but no longer. Her face froze everyone to stone
but with my mirror-shield, cap, and sickle I could deal with her.
When I cut off her head, blood spurted in a fountain.
I had to wash myself in the sea. I had never killed anyone.

I put her head in the bag as I had been told to do
and started home. But I liked flying
and I turned south over Africa.
The desert looked endless — a few palm trees here and there
and towns where there were lakes or rivers.

The worst of it was the bag. Blood kept dripping out of it
and the serpent hair kept writhing.
Several times I almost threw it away.

As I neared Jaffa I saw a girl chained to a rock
the sea dashing over it. Her dark skin gleamed with water.
She wore jewels around her neck and nothing else.
Had she not been beautiful I might have gone on.
It was none of my business what she was doing there.

But then, sliding over the sea a monster appeared
her head twisting around, her body dipping
in and out of the waves. Steam came from her jaws
and scales dangled over her face like seaweed.
Clearly I was destined to do battle.

She was harder to kill than Medusa.
I had to keep flying around her,
invisible, yet in reach of the heavy tail
the spinning jaws. The sea grew bloodier
until at last she sank like a punctured kettle.

I married the maiden, freezing all objections
with the look on Medusa's face
and came home, spellbound the wicked lover,
made the fisherman king. He married my mother
and I became king in Argos.

Now I live idly here, Andromeda beside me
still beautiful, though slow in conversation,
asking myself, was I really a hero?
Or was it the weapons? Could anyone have done it?

After all, what is a kingdom?
The flying, the thrust of battle, the danger,
even the smell of blood, the writhing monsters —
dream or nightmare, then I truly lived.
And was that all? There must be more than this.

Despite All That

she is still telling the tides where to begin.
Under her circle the blood of the lunatic
rises. She calls to the man with the knife.
The hot housewife slides out of the scraps
of the kitchen to the lover under her shadow.
And the seed-burst herring listen for her coming
in the long lurching of the sea.

Water drips from her into the veins of cabbages
and corn silk, and vines send loose tendrils
high toward her crossing. Neither the sunflower
nor day's-eye finds gods more loving
than this enchantress who changes nightly
casting her monthlong circle of chains
over the losers.

Watching the Break-Up

1

Trying to feel sure when you are not sure
is like walking in quicksand, though I never
saw any, or even walked in a swamp
except in the everglades, where paths are everywhere
made of boards. An alligator was
in a pool where fish swam by his mouth
ready for eating, not seeming to care about that.
I met a man who shot 12 crocodiles
one morning on safari. These tears are not
crocodile tears, though I have never seen
a crocodile cry.

2

The clock is a chatterbox, always buzzing about your ear
going rat-a-tat-tat. Bad as a fly.
But you can't swat it. It has to wake you up
at 6 o'clock. Still that's not fair
to the clock, hardworking night and day
like your heart. Both telling your time,
telling your time.
I know of no things less dispensable
than clocks and hearts
even though they break wide open at 6 a.m.
with their alarm.

3

Be undisturbed — you heard only half the story.
But be compassionate — do whatever you can do.
And learn to swim if you live near the ocean.
Many have drowned even in tiny rivers.

Down, Down

I am says the bulldozer
singing brighter than the birds
a thousand birds on a thousand branches
sing no merrier than I

and the crickets' *alas*
the brittle scraping
of a million legs together
or the bellowing of frogs.

I am and send my weighty message
over the hills at daybreak
breaking hills
I am stronger than the mountain.

I push up the knotted roots of sycamores
a hundred summers gathering.
I shake the sunflowers
where the spotted eggs are hiding.

I stamp down this terrace. I descend
to the Pleistocene. This was a lake
then rock. I make it a meadow.
No ages for me. An afternoon is enough.

I am says the bulldozer
and compassed round with music.

Unwinding the Glacier

Not for one moment does this scowler stop
cleaning the monster slope, packing its load
of windowless cathedrals, hulking ships,
untidy monuments.

                         What trees one winter
went down under snow, pack ice burns steadily
across the striae of a widow mountain.
Summer carves its skin with sweat.

Massive and slow we ride these cold windings,
building our Roman road and aqueduct,
riding the rails that stagger as we pass.
Out of its melting pours the clear water — green, pure,
the halo of saints, presenting the piedmont
with its vines and grains — substance of sacrament.

IN MEDITERRANEAN AIR

It was a war that nobody won. Both sides were held in balance, each move checked before it was made, by the brilliant espionage of Count Hugo von S. and the Baroness de B., representing our C.E. countries on the one hand and that of an obscure but dogged agent, whose name has not come to light, on the other. Though he seemed inept, often being glimpsed by the C.E. agents outside their various headquarters, he must have had a superior operation behind him, for our people were never able to shake him off despite constant movement. Unprepossessing, forever merging with the background, even the power(s) he worked for not yet ascertained —

EXCERPT FROM *The Memoirs of Marie Hessenburg-Rothe,* TR. M.K. SHELDON

At the Villa

Who listens to us? Out past the terrace the spy
hides behind Venus's statue
moving nearer, his cheek flat
mottled with rotting marble.
The ebon-eyed goddess
turns black with night.

And the footsteps rustle closer
in a dirty wind that casts over us
grit and a film of leaves. The garden
laid down under heat. The fountains'
statues cracked in the sun. Is he still
flat to Venus's buttocks or is he

wrestling with Adonis by the garden path?
They should have been left together
those two. Let us look at the map now
spread out under the thin torch.
It will draw him, the cheating moth,
antennae spread. His instructions

crackle in the air, signal storm
to some of us. A storm would cool us all
take the sand from the insufferable air, restore
the long look between the statues
down to the gone garden's end, put him in his trenchcoat
drenched anyhow, lurking out there unsheltered.

The Pursuer

He might come through any door —
the thick oak at the top of the curving stair
the painted panels leading to the study
the knobbed iron from the driveway, with its broken lock,
or the French windows opening on the terrace.
Even, God forbid, from the plain door in the passage
leading down dark stone steps to the cellar.

And I, standing in the massive marble hall,
a piece on a chessboard
moving from the square of pale Perlato
to the dark veins of Turquesa.

Those quarries make the whole house cold
with their ungiving surfaces. And the room so bright
it is like a stage, the audience hidden
in the shifty vines of the terrace
or the shadow above the balcony.

For all I know the walls papered with nymphs and fountains
and flowering trees are peopled with watching eyes
and the Venetian mirrors counterfeit.

I pretend to be looking at the statues,
copies of ancient art — Actaeon, Artemis,
Laocoon wreathed in serpents —
while I search for a faint heelmark,
a spot of water, a speck of lint, a shred of paper.

But I find no clue, and logic cannot help me
nor the strained sensing for the hidden breath
the scent of oleander crushed, the faint electric aura
of the body. I must go at once

lock myself incommunicado in the study
take the broad circling stairway into shadow
or the iron doorway leading to the forest.
I have to choose. I could meet him anywhere.

In the Garden

Sun or rain I am out here, shoes overflowing,
or holding to a slice of shadow, while the heat
cracks the ground all around me.
Sweat glues my skin, or else wind
carves my face with granules.

They sit inside with their tea or stroll
after dark on the terrace. There's little shelter,
they have seen to that. If they talk
they find an upstairs room — there's only rotten vines to cling to;
the stones crumble under my toes. I'm no acrobat.

They think they'll outlast me. But they don't dare
leave in the shined Mercedes, ready in the driveway
lest I find the map in the cupboard, the code
under the faded icon in the passage.
They bore one another. The cook never washes his hands.

They'll crack before I do. The khamsin is about to begin —
fifty days of swirling sand. They'll be trapped for sure
with the dirty cook and the rough butler
who shadows them. And I, like a sundial,
patient, enduring, forgiving, in the garden.

The Chase

Sooner or later we must go after them.
Clumsy fools, they can never slip away
without stumbling into a table in the corridor
crashing the lamp. They bring the whole house down
every door opens, lights go on, the butler comes up from the
    wine cellar.

They make a run for it; the car in the driveway is locked
the battery dead, but they get it rolling
and we follow over roaring bridges, through broken
    hedgerows,
turning like wind-devils. Smash over the guardrail.
Their car spirals. They melt into the forest.

We are on foot now, stalking the pine trees
and it's beginning to snow. My hand aches
where the bullet grazed the little finger.
Ice stiffens my town shoes. I am lost.
They have got away once more undeserving.

On the Train

Forget day and night; this is all you can think of.
Forget sleep, breakfast, keeping appointments.
You eat when you can, doze under a tarpaulin,
on trains, in the back seats of rented cars.

Your mind stays on the treadmill.
What it is you are after. You are not even sure,
but it is there somewhere. You have to find it.
That couple ahead — the man with the blue glass eye

the woman in the modish hat, they have hidden it.
The train lurches on. You must rifle the luggage.
What good if they sleep? You wouldn't dare touch them.
You need accomplices, and you haven't any.

You are alone with the search and not much time.
Something must turn your way, you can't trail them forever.
Her gloved hand gestures and you strain to hear.
The glass eye follows you like a periscope.

Incognito

Do they know I have been in the villa?
That I am the mouse that snoops in the corridor
midnight to morning, hearing them joust in bed?
I am the limping man who brings the firewood
my wool cap low on my forehead, my beard gone wild.
I am the plump girl who sells them vegetables;
my head touches the cook's as we lean over the basket.
I was the wisecracking messenger with wilted roses,
the man with the telegram. I carried your bags
when you took the through train to the south.
I was the old gentleman with the cane two seats behind you.
You are such blunderers. Yet you keep it hidden,
what I am after, however I hide myself.

Headquarters

The radio's gone off. I've set the band
at the right time and the number, and nothing comes of it.
A crackle sometimes; it's still alive.
I'm where I should be. The world's disappeared out there.

Why don't they signal? Have they forgotten me?
I tried the telephone, but it kept ringing.
Something's gone wrong.

I can't give up when I am so close to it,
watching the lichens grow on the statues,
sheltering behind them in the sirocco.

I'm the cat that walks at night
sleeps with one eye. I'm a tree. I'm a statue.
I'll get at the secret, though there's no one to take it to.

Three

God, how I envy them! Always together.
The train sways past villages, the dining car
sparkles. They whisper together.
The wine drips amber into their glasses.
He touches her hand in a careless movement,
puts a cigarette in a slim holder,
lights it, passes it to her. They play this game
over and over. It is all for me.

I sit behind the newspaper at the next table —
France-Soir. "Liebling," he says, "liebling,
souviens-toi, l'été dernier sur la plage…"
No one else cares. The waiter a smiling simpleton.

I was careful at the last station.
I boarded without a glance at them.
They know, they know, teasing the scattered table crumbs.
They look for me, watching them, wait for me everywhere.

Outside

Last night the birds outside had their feathers ruffed all right!
Cold as six pigeons! Beer froze on pantry shelves.
Do they know how I feel out here alone?
What if I went away? Who'd care for their pas de deux.
It's only for me
they bolt the iron-studded door at night
pull the rotten drapes near the terrace
and embrace under the lamps by the upstairs window.

It's like marriage. What a waste if I left them!
They pretend to hide messages while I am watching,
or half-burn a paper, throw the rest in the fireplace;
they laugh while I sift their ashes
for a scrap of *Die Zeitung* faintly underlined.
They are my life. I love them. They hate one another.

The Party

I've stayed out here so long my head is ablaze with blossoms.
Stems are growing up all around me bumpy with buds.
It's springtime. My short-wave sputters birdsongs.
The owls whoop all night like lusty nightingales.

The villa is all lit up. Tables swim in flowers —
peonies, ranunculus. I can't keep up with the guests,
generals in full regalia. Bosoms curve under diamonds,
the chandeliers shine, crystal hides the table,
notes pass from hand to hand with the champagne.

Perfume seeps from the terrace in waves
I am about to drown in it! It's been so long!
I'd like to run in, my dusty shoes on the carpet,
snatching up wine, crying *Salut*, and embrace every one
      of them.

The Design

In what design am I, here in the garden —
the garden with its diamond paths
that criss-cross behind hedges,
the flowers settled in their chosen plots
divided by size, function, color even,
the flowers adjusted to conditions:
sun, the minerals of the soil, the frequency of rain —
none deviate, weeds are removed,
all rejuvenate, fertilizing one another
with their special insects — not only bees
but flies, wasps,
even wind. I alone. My function
is merely to watch and wait.

How do I fit in? If I move my foot
I trample on hyacinth, perfume of broken stems,
the petals wetting my boot soles, slippery, yellow.
Pollen lies broken open on the dark green of the stems.
Hostile my foot on the ground, pressing in gentle violence
across the grass. Why am I here?
I am curious. But to break
even the flowers in springtime
argues force, overturning, behavior
I should hate to own.

What is the difference between them and me?
We are for beauty, harmony, joy, utopia
here among the hyacinths, the bells' bloody coral,
the yellow cries of the pistils for rape,

for birdwings, the visits of flying hordes.
Nothing lies between us
but lawns and the cold statues
rotting by the old walls.

I have imagined a paradise where no serpent enters
without apples hidden under
the cushions of the parlor, or under
the marble set at tangents in the gallery.
Yet we stand here on both sides of the wall
listening to one another. Our inner states
of love, happiness — it is a strain to bear all this.
Happiness itself is a terror.
I can only conclude with the secret:
it is the wall of thorns; it is the fruit in the parlor;
it is the flight and the chase; it is the disillusion;
it is what we are all afraid of.

After Exile

It was not the dream that did it.
It only reflected
the serpent of power rising
from the roots of earth
into the head where the hair
flew out like sprays of a flowering tree.
Blossoms falling wherever the feet
half-touched the ground
the girl with new-risen breasts
running through doorways
into the green garden
where trees grew overnight
placing themselves in trim rows
and the blooms of azaleas, acacia,
and pomegranate split the air with color,
whole skies of blooms covered the ground
but it was the fountain that rose like a serpent
ricocheted over every tendril of the green garden.

The Turn

Like lying down for winter, all life
drained — mud at the base of a pool —
scum freezing over — the bones bent like ribbons
around the limp center
the saints locked in their chambers
saying I am nothing.

Morning not a clatter of bird notes and wings
but a sour taste and voices,
no reasons to go or stay, only to keep the sky
and earth apart. Caught in the knuckled hand
a fistful of clay.

This is when it turns, begins to shoot
up the green brace that breaks open the hand
and suddenly into the white light
of ordinary morning like a reed
or a vine or a tree that will scratch at heaven.

Listening to Color

Now that blue has had its say
has told its winds, wall, sick
sky even, I can listen to white

sweet poison flowers   hedge autumn
under a sky white at the edges
like faded paper. My message keeps

turning to yellow where few leaves
set up first fires over branches
tips of flames only, nothing here finished yet.

FROM

Dreaming the Garden

2000

Returning Once More

Be thankful now that you have survived
have come back to tell from a miry cave
filled with hothouse fronds that sway
and bend greedy coxcombs above you,
that down some road you stumble back to morning

That the plants here are less bloodthirsty
dropping their leaves in their own style
as autumn requires, the skinny branches
willy-nilly giving up their gold
and stretching out to lacerate the sky.

And having returned from one more journey
give thanks that there are some to welcome you
with brief attention, busy with their mornings
(the sun runs cold among the sidewalk leaves
red berries open up their harvest)

And for the blond hair and the grey
for the tink-a-tunk in the kitchen
the squirrel clucking among the branches, the boy
on the yellow bicycle, the pulse of a neighbor's hammer
convincing you this is the true and solid day.

Waiting for Rain

We have waited one hundred sixty-seven days
for rain. May into November.
Now we have gathered firewood by the door
in a sheltered place, where bulbs try to break
the crusts of the clay.
167 days. We put the tools in the shed
and at night listen.
The highway rustles like wind.
The wind blows hard leaves over the roof
and we hear the first false drops.
The world is as dry as ever.

It will come, it will come
while we are sleeping.
We will move in our dreams
where a lover has kissed us
whom we have never seen.
We will open our closet doors
and gold will fall over the worn shapes of our shoes
onto the floor.

Wherever we go we will find silver.
We will be green and olive
and our garden
will shake off the dust of summer.
The air will be clean again.
We will waken to rain so soft
we cannot quite hear it
but we will know, we will know:
we have been waiting for rain.

Mountain Poems

1

It's time we got to the mountains
they've been waiting
a long time.
The granite's cracked
and the lichen
has taken the pinetrees.
The stream's almost empty.
The hawks have gone.

2

It's hard
talking the mountain
into anything.
Say *come down here* —
at once!
A few small stones
down the alluvium,
the stream quickens
bringing granules,
and the leaves gyrate
up and down.
It's slow going.
You haven't time to wait.

3

Wait
rock says
wait

hurry down
says stream
run

up you go
says wind
way high

I can't go
says ground
I have all this
to eat.

4

Say
the flowers on that hillside
are stars
or waves
or tents or ribbons
or bursts of sun,

say they're light
or courage
or remembrance.

They still keep nodding.

5

Nor yet begun
the scrawny branches where the buds
crouch in hard cases.
The world's gone grey.

The ground huddles in sun
no berries, no passing birds.
The sky limps by.
Only absence keeps its name.

6

Into this, into this
slowly
movement too small to see
to count
but into this
lifting
sure as the spiral
thrusts
the heaviest base
the load moves up
the sky propped
with banners
the mountain flattening
under blue.

Childhood

For each a golden age. The trees brimming
with leaves, the garden's mysterious flowers —
sweet-scented nicotiana, nasturtiums in a pool of sunlight,
mint under the faucet drip — an enclosure
where English walnuts sent long, pollen-dropping blooms
over the driveway. Freesias marched across the lawn
through crimson bells. Sweet peas
climbed by the window.

Hard times, and the gleaners
followed the walnut harvest, or in spring
picked mustard from the fields. Wanderers — hungry men —
came to the back door.

The orchard flung down more than we wanted —
first plums, then peaches, oranges, persimmons,
and the garden shot up scalloped squash
green beans, tomatoes, a profusion.

Sundays we sat among uncles and aunts,
lingered round the oak table, heavy with bounty,
in the far-off age, golden, encircled,
the world falling apart, armies beginning to move.

DREAMING THE GARDEN

It is so comfortable there in the garden.
You can wear an old toga.

PLINY THE YOUNGER

The aesthetics of an age appear in all the arts, and
one can find striking parallels among them. See how
the square straight beds of the Renaissance garden,
resembling in form the square poetic stanzas of the
period, gave way to the curved borders and wander-
ing edges of artificial lakes in the Romantic period
at the same time that Wordsworth wrote in long over-
lapping lines of mists and ruins and vine-covered
cottages. And the poems of the eighteenth century
are filled with nymphs and gods while their temples
were built in gardens.

And in the garden, which is a living thing, one
can find parallels to the life of the artist: the theory
under which the poet works, the joys and hopes at
the beginning, the set-backs and struggles, just as
the garden shifts, through neglect, heat and cold,
torrents of rain, vandals. All change the life of the
garden, just as they do the life of the artist.

M.C. WROCKSTON,
The Garden and Other Arts (1869)

Dreaming the Garden

1

It must first of all be fun.
There must be an air of insouciance,
of *je ne sais quoi* about it.
Someone else has already moved the stones,
limed the soil. You have only to turn
the shovel lightly. The rains have left
moisture, but not too much.
You plan the lawn, sloping to the terrace,
the marble balustrades, cracks hidden
under the wash of plumbago.
You are half down the slope. Beyond
are oaks and beech trees surrounding the view
of the lake. Beyond it — the lake —
are mountains — green overlaying the hidden villas.
A single boat loiters among lily pads.

But there is work to do.
You put the shovel deep in and turn
up humus, earthworms, a bulb or two
beginning to send a green shaft skyward.
By the lake, back from the point where the
trees obscure the boat now
a cluster of statues watches the view
from atop the columned wall
above the anchorage.
The boat will be heading this way.

To your left past the maze
the lawn edged by nymphs hip-deep in azaleas,
moves toward the folly.
Beside the stairs to the terrace
geraniums flow out of their vases, pink and lavender.
Off toward the south, aisles of lantana
and cannas, the air harsh where the sun
drags the strong scent from the strident blooms.
But on the right, the cascade
plunges through pools, descends in shallow falls
noisy as a brook. Grottoes and archways span and interrupt.
Dolphins rise from the pool
and a great shell collects
the last outflow, from which it vanishes.

You have done so much this morning —
two shovelfuls of earth. The third
leads to the clipped ilex on the terrace.
Diamonds, circles of low hedge
hold bouquets. The square pool marks
the heart. Beyond,
water and light make the statues move,
the sky a lake of clouds under the arches by
the shell. You walk under the falling tide
with the nymphs who hold spirals of shells
wreathed in ivy.
You go up the water stairs. Cascades rush by
on either hand. Shade dapples the path.
You reach the main pool:
against the hillside a grove,
in the grove the goddess
white, serious, stone, follows the deer
at the edge of the glade. You have come just in time.

2

Start with the bounds. What's to go out or stay.
The view you'll keep, the lake, the fading ranges.
Columns of cypress shield the western slope,
as for the south, arrange a grove of olives.
On the north, white oleander
can form a wall beside the avenue.
Over the walk you put an arch of vines.
You must be firm with space. Even the sky
becomes your own.

Divide the sky, let it be lanes or views,
parterres, or rounds of blue above the pool.
Cut it with branches, winter-white, in shapes
of leaded glass, break it with scattered leaves
into shimmering drops, or panes
between the arches of the hedge, or dark with lines
or circles from your vista under the trees.
You've set the bounds, laid out the earth and sky.
Whatever you do, things will not stay this way.

3

It helps if you have something old
to set among the hedges:
say a column topped by a statue of Ceres,
behind her a rondure of privet,
or a sundial on a post of white marble
in the circle of lawn.
Where that pile of native stone backs the fountain
a group of nymphs, sporting jets of spray
from the cascade hidden behind the potting shed.
Some urns of terra cotta
can hold salvia, the yellow anthers bright in sun.

Not too much color though.
Let the subtle glow of marble hold your attention.

If you are fortunate, you will find fragments —
a broken head of an emperor
the pediment of an altar
or, truly blessed, a faun
tangled in grape leaves.
Set him among boxes of orange
against the ilex hedge,
the gravel path widening before him.
Even a few broken shards
will enhance the wall behind the fountain.

The past must be used —
the sarcophagi flaunting geraniums —
and where the wood overtakes you, a path
through the overgrown laurel
the tangle of oak and acacia
always at war with one another.

4

It rains. The lake drowns in haze.
The grove beside it is a distant country.
Fog moves in billows like nymphs escaped from the fountains,
their white drapes drawn about them.
Rain shoots from the downspouts, jets from the mouths
        of gargoyles,
or rolls off the roof, splashing and rebounding.
The terrace is a pool catching the gush of waters
from the mouths of eagles, the vases of naiads,
the horse-maned dolphins of the seagod.
The villa is a fountain, where you swim like a minnow
in the green light of leaves dripping their cascades.

The sky darkens. It is a grotto
filled with swaying moss, the dark niches holding satyrs
grinning as they wave obscene fingers
or sneer at you from the green solace of vines.
The terrace where you dug is mud; it melts
sliding down the water stairs
between the troughs where freshets leap
from banks of honeysuckle.
Water runs between the balustrades
in waterfalls that merge
like the outflow of a thousand breasts
into the great pool on the lower terrace
where the hedge floats like a carved isthmus
among islands of clipped lavender.
Water flows from the boughs of the pine trees
pours from the laurels, circles the oranges, dangles in
narrow streams from the walnuts.
The lake must be rising among the oak trees
making a water temple of the columns by the landing.
The statues gaze at their reflections
pocked by descending drops.
You hear the counterpoint of the shattering cascade
off the edge of the roof, the tattoos of rain,
a slow drip, drop, somewhere it shouldn't be.
The birds have taken to cover.
You hear no sound
but the steady water music of the garden.

5

But it must make sense. The mad cascade
the storm dropped yesterday has destroyed the parterres.
They are sunk in mud. The stairways slipping with dirt
      and leaves.

Everything drips — the eaves, the edges of trees, the hedges.
It was more than a water garden, a meeting of too many streams.
After a day of sun, you can clean out the path
wash off the terraces, put drains where streams carried away
        the soil.

But today while the clouds decide whether to go or stay
get to details. What is the garden made of?
Planes, levels, paving, paths, trees and hedges,
low plantings and high, sun and shade, color and light.

Down by the lake already there are beeches and oaks,
a drift of wild cyclamen. Farther up for sun
plant a spread of lantana, a border of lilies,
on the terrace end, magnolias; around the reflecting pool
urns of geraniums, plumbago, purple
bougainvillea, vases of lemon set on balustrades
and hedges of laurel, cypress, holly.
For the old walls, jasmine, clematis, honeysuckle, roses
beside iris and loquat, oleanders, mandarins.
For autumn color liquidambars, persimmons, against the
        pine trees.
Pomegranate and flowering thyme,
lavender, shrub roses, fuchsias
and wisteria on the steeper banks.
You will want mimosa and orange trees
the acrid scent of alders by the stream.

But your list is already too long
and you've left no room for the kitchen garden.
You have forgotten the plan, the cool laying out of the ground.
You have overwhelmed the garden, unthinking as any god.

Early snow, unexpected, falls on the terraces.
The flakes are large and soft, they scatter on the path
like cherry blooms by the kitchen garden.
You go through the gate to the canal.
There puzzled swans break a skim of ice
as they glide to shore. From the bare limbs of the river birch
snow drops in gouts on your shoulders. The sky lightens
as you cross the bridge. Will you try the maze?
But the sky lowers again. You might be lost there
and the great clots of snow falling faster.
You walk through the orchard with its expected
peach, pear, apple, plum, the figs espaliered on the wall
next the topiary garden, now melting stone
where the careful diamonds hide their secrets.
It is getting colder, and the wind
penetrates the hedges, but you have still
the ballroom lying in two long fields
empty with a desolate sound.
It is too vast. You must get to shelter.
You hurry past pillars of snow
their circles etched in ice.
You wander from the path, tripping on borders.
The snow falls faster; you wander among boxwood.
Are you back in the maze? You cross under an arch
stumble among stones. You crawl under the aerial hedge
blunder down stairs toward the water.
It has vanished along with the swans
with the redbud, river oak, magnolias,
the kitchen garden, the ice house, and the mount
and the meadow beyond the fences.

The house is gone and the stable
and there is nothing but a white wall
moving around you. Nothing but snow and silence.

6

You must get back to the plan
the central theme, the axis of the garden
that great effect each part must be subject to.
You can pull it together
by a great stairway perhaps,
breaking across the terraces, holding them like a knot
around a bundle.
Or a major prospect. You must frame the view
between windows of laurel
or a balustrade at the edge of the terrace.
Don't let it simply slide away.

If the terrain allows, you may put a central walk
down to the lake. The slope will give you streams
from the upper cascade, a suite of stairs and lawns and pools,
that rise in fountains — a dolphin or seahorse, a goddess
surrounded by naiads, or an arched tower
from which the flow thunders into whirlpools.
At angles to the axis will be corridors
between gardens of cypress, holm oak, chestnut, or cedar;
these passages lead into gardens
each with its focus — statue, flower bed, sundial.

Or let the main path be a corridor
between privet; the clipped alleyways
lead to quiet openings beside lilyponds.
Or a central fountain, or a stair uphill
to a portico over the blue paving of the lake

with its grand vista fronting the water,
the terrace leading to the belvedere,
formal and open, inviting by its long straight paths
the gaiety of sunlight, the mock of shadow,
the white admonition of the statues.

7

Things can get so easily out of hand.
Whatever you do, you must keep order.
Here where the horses broke through things have gone to ruin.
Refugees camped here, the statues are lost
or broken. The lilies dragged from the pond
where they washed their rags and their children.
They burned the hedges for firewood
cooking thin gruel, warming their hands,
blackening the wall behind the fires.
It was frosty those nights. The temple of Demeter
hung with bedclothes to keep out the wind,
her columns slant with ropes,
the goddess fallen. Boots chipped her fingers,
her torch carried away, her basket broken.

Up by the terrace wall some spread their tents
with poles of cut cypress. They thatched them with branches.
Boys pushed the urns from the terrace
carved their names on the wall.
Sheep and goats nibbled the thyme of the parterre
ate the leaves of hydrangeas;
and cows tethered to the columns of the balustrades
pulled them out like ragged teeth.
The garden disappeared in mud and slime
and the trample of feet.
But the old ilexes remain

their twisted roots hold the rifts of a wall
built by the emperor. This was ruin before.

Now you begin.

8

Yes, it is getting harder.
The easy part was beginning
dreaming the garden, but it is midday
and there's much to do
more perhaps than you are able.
The ground where you dig has become harder,
the tangle of laurel beyond keeps out sunlight.
You stand on the long terrace
where the ground was trampled
under so many feet.
When you began, it did not seem this way
the shovel went into the loam, into the soft
leavings of leaves.
                    The lake is farther away
and the boat has disappeared.
The cloud coming up from the west
throws a shadow on the lake;
it goes dull like a piece of chiseled slate.
Rain will bring mud; you'd better dig
while there is time. You look at the stains
where fire burned the wall,
the graffiti, and the torn balustrades.
Your arms ache. You must bring leaves
and manure, gravel for paths.
You started so bravely. All you did was dream.
You dreamed the garden. Start now.
There is time.

Tomorrow you can put up the statues
mend the broken urns, take another look
at the long vista you first thought of.

9 DESERTED GARDEN

This garden needs you. Between its walls
a central path, iris and asters, pear trees in rows
and the blue of wisteria over the gateway.
But beyond the gate, matted grass and weeds
overrun the paths, splash against walls
and ivy thickens over the fallen columns.
Once there were laurels here, now only traces
of ruined walkways. The deserted terrace
overlooks the sea gate and the broken hedges
where the white, deep-rooted morning glory sprawls over
        broken rubble.

You long to pull at the weeds, clear out the paths,
cut the thicket of myrtle, set up the columns,
plant foxgloves and asters, rosemary, marigolds,
put lemon against the walls, trim the broken hedges
and sit at evening ·
looking over the garden and the wall
where the warm blooms mingle with wind from the sea.

But it doesn't belong to you. Not for you to untangle
the smother of green, you with your hillside
waiting, deserted, unfinished, as you mourn for this
        lost garden.

DREAMING THE WINTER GARDEN (II)

It is midmorning.
You are resting on the terrace
the broad walk paved in sun
yet chill. It is January
and the wind blows down from the mountains
beyond the garden. On their peaks, snow,
but here the earth begins to put on color.

You sip the coffee so kindly sent from the house behind you
set your cup on the wrought-iron table —
the hostess has thought of that (you have never seen her) —
and look over the lawn toward the statue —
Louis the Fifteenth listening to Cupid.
The king stands — or sits — from here you can't be sure
under a pediment, a simple triangle
held up by columns. Is there a roof as well?
One day you must stroll across that mile of lawn,
but now the sun has disappeared, and the terrace
feels the bite of wind.
You walk a few paces to the balustrade
set with the usual urns, these without flowers,
closed at the top, of a tender stone
that weathers (some of the garlands are broken)
grand nevertheless. At the end of the paving
three dogs attack a boar. One clings
to the underbelly. The others climb on his back
or snap at his jowls. It is a draw
at the moment, and as yet no blood,
only the green velvet of verdigris, like a net over the scene
as though it is happening in a dream. You look away

but in the same green and opposite
the dogs have cornered a deer and seem to be winning.
Noble stag! you cry, but what can you tell it,
mired in green as it is, forever in combat.
You move toward the rose garden.
A hedge shields you from the north
but wind rattles through the bare branches
at the top of the arbor.
You take shelter under the giant oaks
among the camellias, deep pink and light, the yellow
stamens like eyes watching where you go,
past the dolphin fountain, where the wind blows spray,
across the path to the safe shelter of the trees again.
And back over the open lawn to the terrace,
broad, swept clean, empty, the table gone, the urns
flaking, the beasts still tearing one another.

10

It is too cold to work.
No one cares anyway you tell yourself.
It's your garden, if it lies
forever undone, that's your business.
It's only for joy. You are tired
of the stubborn limbs all greedy for light
knotting themselves, choking one another.
The ground, baked hard, cracking in the sun,
and the creatures around and underground
waiting for something to grow.
Birds mock you from the trees, daring you like the others.

The lake has gone down to a stinking pool
edged with mud. The boat rots on the shore,
the seams break open in air, weeds hold the anchor chain

and the sky is neither sun nor cloud
but brown at the edges, pale at the center,
and a thick haze fills the gaps between the mountains.

If anyone cared, you repeat,
you might untangle the wood, close up the passageways
to the underground, rip out the vines
that strangle the trees, the thorny weeds, if anyone,
you say again, if anyone.

11

The garden is only for you. It is a shell
in which you live. It is a wall
to keep you from the world. You are the center.
Not the pool where dryads
pour water forever in meaningless gestures,
nor the stairs with stone balustrades
where eagles spread their useless wings of stone
nor the clipped alley between cypress hedges.

You are the garden. Let it circle round you.
You are the heart of the maze, where the laurel
draws its own pyramid, shakes out its limbs
overhangs the path and takes the form of trees.
Leave Daphne there
her freed limbs shaking in the autumn wind.
See the colors of autumn — chrysanthemums, asters,
the lawn covered with leaves where yellow and red
rain from the trees, and for your pleasure
the black-crested quail wander over the lawns.

The boat drifts farther away; it is leaving
and flocks of traveling common birds feast on the red berries.

The orange trees
set here and there forget the terraces
and the path curves away among the pine trees.
You are inside the garden, and it takes your form.
It is real now, not a plan, not even a vista,
but a warm wall in winter, an old coat thrown around you.

The Fountain

You must remember never to offend the gods
by being too sure of anything.
Think of Niobe, how she grew in pride
watching her seven tall sons and seven fair daughters.

Who would not? Having created such
superb heads set on the pure column
of the neck, the long hair glistening in the sun
and their voices musical as water

in a bright stream rippling over rocks —
the archer, the runner, the studious,
the orator, the weaver, the gatherer of garlands,
one with his horse, another at the lyre.

Wherever she looked she saw the gold
limbs of her children, strong
in the sun, their laughter
beyond the sounds of the strings, even the chords

Orpheus struck before he lost his bride
before he disobeyed the charge of Hades
and looked back into the dark
where Arachne in a still corner wove

over and over the stories of the gods
and their offenses, how Hades caught
Persephone, and Leto's son
killed one by one the children of Niobe.

Mind

It's a web.
Leaves rot in the passage way,
feathers, hollows of flies —
companions. They're all there.
I'm walking over my past.
It's my house, my bridge.
My panel of eyes glim the future
eight hands might grasp.
It's meat and drink, meat and drink
I collect. The rest falls through.

Wind, though, I like it.
A fresh thought
opens the web,
it bleeds old fragments
and frets away ravel.

There's left only me.
Out of myself the clean thread —
the long floats catch somewhere —
the swing, the swinging!

MAKERS

The Sword

I made the sword.
Here in the fire I plunged the steel
white hot bearing the beat of the apprentice's
hammers, one-two-three over and over
on the steel bar — over and over the firing
the beating of hammers till the bar is dense
with the struggle, and I bend it again and again.
Over and over the pounding, the cutting, the bending,
layer on layer the crude bar resists me.

I have given it courage. It has held day and night
against heat, against pounding. At last I have shaped it,
hardened its edges.
It becomes a mirror of my hand hardened in fire

with the metal that resists and is beaten
folded and beaten to the luster
of the still pond that is windless
that carries one gold curving branch in its center
spread with the gold leaves of springtime
and waiting
to bring you this mirror, this hardness, this ardor of
      hammering home.

The Weaver

I am the weaver.
Before the last frosts I planted the seeds
covered with straw from the reeds by the river.
Green rising under the moon in springtime
the jagged long leaves lifting a tide around me.

In summer the blue seeds appeared
grew into harvest, and the blue of indigo
rose in the water when the cloth I had woven
took the color of sky, took the azure of evening,
took the darkness of blue night without stars.

Shining, the cloth that I carried
down to the river stones, carefully washing
the dross from the workroom, leaving blue
caught as the clear afternoon
looking down on the river.

The sedges dripped toward the water, dipped in blue
dropped from the sky, and the broad channel
ran from the cloth over the blue rocks
under the sky that would darken
into still ponds where the frogs turned
to blue statues in cold streams of midnight.

I have woven through springtime
at dawn at my shuttle; now the blue sky
dries in my yard. This blue will not fade.
It will darken to midnight. It will tell

of the river; it will speak of the weaver. It will
last you a hundred years
out of myself, out of the sky and river woven.

The Bell

I am the bell.
I am from earth and fire.
Now the bronze gleams round my shoulder.
I hold your prayers, burned to ash
and sent to the skies with my echoing.

I echo your names and the names of god.
Further and further the ring widens
grows fainter, never dies away
but quivers alone at the edge of the hills
caught like night's fog below the mountains.

Long and deep the hollow within me
where the sound comes to birth
where the shudder first catches
the bronze at my side, vibrates and travels
round and round my surface like the thongs

of a sling whirled in air till it borrows
flight from its circling, and the sound
flies out, while the trees
flutter with birds flung like notes
to the wind, and the river catches
my singing sound and the wind carries
my notes like the names of the gods over and over.

At the Vernal Equinox

Lord, come again in these your premises
in our hills where the sunflower opens morning
stretching toward that center where we bend.

Before us you have laid your implements:
the sun heaps up for us bales of new leaves,
vines loop over the trees their terraces.

The birds forgive us. The hawk up there
perfects the wind. The flicker proves the woods.
The linnet, hopeful, plants her little nest
in every thicket, and the world's

giddy with sunflowers, that open up dark
eyes to gaze into the pit of heaven
to be the crown gentle on the head of common things.

The Old Couple

The goose noticed them first, the travelers,
strangers most likely, for they had passed the town
and it was close to evening.
I shaded my eyes while the goose continued
a garrulous hissing and the old man
put down his hoe and stood beside me watching.

We waited still as two old trees. The strangers
took their time coming up hill, where the stones
still held the day's heat, let it out warmly,
the tall one pushing hard against his staff,
the other, smaller, in a battered cloak
was light of foot and fairly danced beside him.

The gods have told us to entertain strangers
lest we turn a god from the door,
but two men less like gods I have not seen.
The goose Miranda, always a judge of character,
made for them as they came, and the small one
kicked her away with his foot roughly.

I will remember always the scowling face
ducking under the lintel, the slow stride
that took up half the room
the big man, tall as an oak, his staff
more like a club. His black beard shone.
He looked younger here than he seemed in the distance.

Robbers or just tired travelers, I knew
we must welcome them. I shook a cloth
out over the wicker couch. The goose kept hissing
and a wind outside fussed in the oleanders.
I blew on the cool ashes of the fire
bringing up sparks, threw in leaves and branches.

The husband brought them water to wash in
and went outside for greens — spinach and turniptops
and early mustard. The kettle boiling
I added the greens and a big piece of bacon
from the flitch in the chimney. I wiped the old table
with mint and rosemary. The eggs cooked in the ashes.

The bench covered with cloth and the table
set with radishes, goat cheese, eggs, pickled berries,
olives from the tree in the dooryard
and the hot stew of herbs. But the strangers
seemed hungry enough for a roast ox
or a spring lamb from the neighbor's pasture.

To the gods, said the old man, and he
poured wine into the clay cups — wine
from our own vines, not rare, but pleasant enough.
The dark traveler smiled, though slightly, like the sun-
light after thunder. The fair one seemed hiding a secret
about to fly from his mocking lips.

He had traveled far, that one, had seen the world
even the palaces of Thessaly and Ithaca
where the sun sinks, and the island of Crete
and farther south even, the land of the Nile

where the crocodiles live, and Rhodes
and the rocky temples of Attica.

The wine tasted better than usual. The dark beard smiled
though wily as ever. Twice the old man rose
to fill the pitcher, but it stayed full enough.
Even the apples and honey that finished the meal
tasted different from every day — and better.

Meanwhile the tattered cape was growing brighter
seemingly newer and there were the sparks
one sees in dry weather when a cloth is shaken.
I noticed the bearded one looked taller
as he sat on the bench, his head almost touching the thatch.
Wine does things sometimes, even a drink or two.

It was impossible. The wine bowl kept brimming
no matter how much we drank. The two growing taller
and beginning to shine. *These are gods*
whispered the old man suddenly, *we must sacrifice.*
The goose must be killed before them.

But the silly goose had no mind for that.
We couldn't catch her. She settled next to the strangers.
Let her go, they said. *We can do better.*
You know the rest, the flood that killed the villagers,
the cottage changed to a temple and we its guardians,
and the goose getting fat on the sacred grain.

But I miss the old ways. We were used to the cottage,
the walls and roof close around us. These high columns
and the gold roof are all right for gods,

we were content where we were. There was plenty
for an old couple wrinkled as tree bark, hands spotted
    and gnarled,
and the vines of the good earth already reaching up for us.

Goat Dancer

When I was young I followed the goats to pasture
prodding old Chronos, though there was time
and nothing to do but watch the rise and fall of their beards
and the kids leaping in the spring, drinking
at the thin stream in summer, when we crossed
on the way to a higher meadow.
It was always good weather, and the evening
brought us down again and again in a rhythm
of going and coming under the oak trees.

I came to another country. The astrologer
found a new name for me. I lived under other stars
by another sea, and I have grown old here.
But I remember Chronos and Flower and Nicolas
and I have come back to them, my companions.

I spring like a kid in the evening
leaping and twisting while the goats circle round
and watch, and old Buttercup twirls on her hind legs,
as if they too remember the enchanted country.

Crisis

Whatever this is, you have only this moment to do it in.
You must decide. The shadow of the hawk
rumples over the grass, splits on sharp stones;
the wave hangs motionless
spitting at the stiff edge, ready.

Only this between the descent
through the broken air, the water already
roaring and the knife-edge beak
breaking over the grassy shore.

Be brief. It is time to put out a hand
against the hawk, the wave.
Can you no longer hear
the shadow rattle the grass, the sea dividing —

caught like a stone in the hawk's eye, the tunnel of water,
the ice wall of this unchangeable moment.

The Woman on the Island

I have tried to tell you how it was on the island,
left alone, the village deserted, the path
growing high with grasses,
the days passed in watching.

Always the same, the same gulls
haunting the rock face, their white wings
hovering over the shallows,
their cries constant as the sea's mutterings.

Once in a while I climbed the cliff by the shore
and watched for the ship that was sure to come.
But the years passed like leaves, where I recorded the seasons.
Notch after notch, first the moons, then the changes
from green spring to summer
to the fogs of autumn and the cold
wind bringing rain.

Still, sometimes I looked out over the sea
past the coastal shallows, where the swells
rose like the gray humps of whales
going southward in springtime.

I forgot the moons, then the seasons.
Only the years returned. I forgot the look
of the sea where it lay in its own
blue vast widening circle round the island.

365 Poems

They will be floating from my mouth like doves
like bright scarves from the sleeves of the magician.
Look, I am spinning five of them over my head.
It has been a bad dream when I
forgot to twirl one like a flag every day,
to walk into town like a parade
with flutes and drums, with timbrels.
They will be chariots drawn by lions.
They will be gazelles and leopards.
They will fly around me like a flock of birds.
They will be my traveling companions.
They will gnaw at me day and night
like minnows, or devour me whole like the whale.
I will stand among them as among trees of a forest,
calling, these are all mine!
They will tell me secrets.
Wherever I go like the roll of drums,
salvos of guns, rockets kindling the air,
they will arrive day and night.
I will beg them to go away.
They will torment me like gnats,
swoop by like hawks at noon, bewilder my dreams at evening.
They will say, welcome home.

About the Author

ANN STANFORD (1916–1987) was born in La Habra and lived her whole life in California. She was awarded a scholarship to Stanford University, where she was associated with the group of young poets surrounding Yvor Winters in the late thirties. She received her Ph.D. in English Literature from the University of California, Los Angeles. From 1962 to 1985, Stanford taught literature and writing at California State University, Northridge. She was the first woman to be named Professor of the Year in the California State system in 1974. Her poems appeared frequently in such journals as *The New Yorker, The Atlantic Monthly, Poetry,* and *The New Republic,* and she also wrote essays on poets and poetry for a number of scholarly journals. In 1970 her verse translation of *The Bhagavad Gita* was published, followed by, in 1972, her anthology *The Women Poets in English,* the first comprehensive collection of poetry by women.

Ann Stanford received many awards for her poetry, among them the Shelley Memorial Award, an Award for Literature from the National Institute of Arts and Letters, and the Di Castagnola Award of the Poetry Society of America. Stanford was the recipient of two National Endowment for the Arts grants and one National Endowment for the Humanities grant, as well as two silver medals for poetry from the Commonwealth Club of California. She was poetry consultant for the Huntington Library, an officer of the Poetry Society of America and of the Associated Writing Programs, poetry editor for *The Los Angeles Times* from 1957 to 1967, and chairperson of the Pulitzer Prize Committee for Poetry in 1984. After her death, the Ann Stanford Poetry Prize, sponsored by the University of Southern California, was created in her honor.

About the Editors

MAXINE SCATES is the author of *Toluca Street* (University of Pittsburgh Press, 1989). Her poems have appeared widely in such journals as *AGNI, The American Poetry Review, Antioch Review,* and ZYZZYVA. She has taught poetry at Lewis and Clark and Reed Colleges and currently teaches at the Mountain Writers Center in Portland, Oregon. Originally from Los Angeles, she has lived in Eugene, Oregon, since 1973.

DAVID TRINIDAD's books include *Plasticville* (Turtle Point Press, 2000); *Answer Song* (High Risk Books, 1994); *Hand Over Heart: Poems 1981–1988* (Amethyst Press, 1991); and *Pavane* (Sherwood Press, 1981). He currently teaches poetry at Rutgers University and is a member of the core faculty in the M.F.A. program at The New School. Originally from Los Angeles, Trinidad has lived in New York City since 1988.

Copper Canyon Press wishes to acknowledge the support of
Lannan Foundation in funding the publication and distribution
of exceptional literary works.

LANNAN LITERARY SELECTIONS 2001

Hayden Carruth, *Doctor Jazz*

Norman Dubie, *The Mercy Seat:
Collected & New Poems, 1967–2001*

Theodore Roethke, *On Poetry & Craft*

Ann Stanford, *Holding Our Own:
The Selected Poems of Ann Stanford*

Mónica de la Torre & Michael Wiegers, editors,
Reversible Monuments: Contemporary Mexican Poetry

For more on the Lannan Literary Selections,
visit our web site:

www.coppercanyonpress.org

This book is set in Electra, created by American typographer and book designer W.A. Dwiggins in 1935. The dingbats are also his designs. The titles are set in Phaistos, designed by David Berlow and Just van Rossum, inspired by Rudolf Koch's 1922 typeface Locarno. Book design and composition by Valerie Brewster, Scribe Typography. Printed on archival-quality Glatfelter Author's Text by McNaughton & Gunn, Inc.

www.smpl.org